D0435134

Mia America / isona

11-10-19

The Arab Spring Uprisings

Hal Marcovitz

Bruno Leone
Series Consultant

ReferencePoint Press®

San Diego, CA

© 2014 ReferencePoint Press, Inc.
Printed in the United States

For more information, contact:
ReferencePoint Press, Inc.
PO Box 27779
San Diego, CA 92198
www. ReferencePointPress.com

LIBRARY OF CONGRESS CATALOGING-IN-PUBLICATION DATA

Marcovitz, Hal.
  The Arab spring uprisings / by Hal Marcovitz.
    pages cm. — (Understanding world history series)
  Includes bibliographical references and index.
  ISBN-13: 978-1-60152-630-4 (hardback)
  ISBN-10: 1-60152-630-X (hardback)
  1. Arab Spring, 2010- 2. Arab countries—Politics and government—21st century. 3. Middle East—Politics and government—21st century. I. Title.
  JQ1850.A91M368 2014
  909'.097492708312—dc23
                                                                  2013034897

Contents

Foreword

When the Puritans first emigrated from England to America in 1630, they believed that their journey was blessed by a covenant between themselves and God. By the terms of that covenant they agreed to establish a community in the New World dedicated to what they believed was the true Christian faith. God, in turn, would reward their fidelity by making certain that they and their descendants would always experience his protection and enjoy material prosperity. Moreover, the Lord guaranteed that their land would be seen as a shining beacon—or in their words, a "city upon a hill,"—which the rest of the world would view with admiration and respect. By embracing this notion that God could and would shower his favor and special blessings upon them, the Puritans were adopting the providential philosophy of history—meaning that history is the unfolding of a plan established or guided by a higher intelligence.

The concept of intercession by a divine power is only one of many explanations of the driving forces of world history. Historians and philosophers alike have subscribed to numerous other ideas. For example, the ancient Greeks and Romans argued that history is cyclical. Nations and civilizations, according to these ancients of the Western world, rise and fall in unpredictable cycles; the only certainty is that these cycles will persist throughout an endless future. The German historian Oswald Spengler (1880–1936) echoed the ancients to some degree in his controversial study *The Decline of the West*. Spengler asserted that all civilizations inevitably pass through stages comparable to the life span of a person: childhood, youth, adulthood, old age, and, eventually, death. As the title of his work implies, Western civilization is currently entering its final stage.

Joining those who see purpose and direction in history are thinkers who completely reject the idea of meaning or certainty. Rather, they reason that since there are far too many random and unseen factors at work on the earth, historians would be unwise to endorse historical predictability of any type. Warfare (both nuclear and conventional), plagues, earthquakes, tsunamis, meteor showers, and other catastrophic world-changing events have loomed large throughout history and prehistory. In his essay "A Free Man's Worship," philosopher and mathematician Bertrand Russell (1872–1970) supported this argument, which many refer to as the nihilist or chaos theory of history. According to Russell, history follows no preordained path. Rather, the earth itself and all life on earth resulted from, as Russell describes it, an "accidental collocation of atoms." Based on this premise, he pessimistically concluded that all human achievement will eventually be "buried beneath the debris of a universe in ruins."

Whether history does or does not have an underlying purpose, historians, journalists, and countless others have nonetheless left behind a record of human activity tracing back nearly 6,000 years. From the dawn of the great ancient Near Eastern civilizations of Mesopotamia and Egypt to the modern economic and military behemoths China and the United States, humanity's deeds and misdeeds have been and continue to be monitored and recorded. The distinguished British scholar Arnold Toynbee (1889–1975), in his widely acclaimed twelve-volume work entitled *A Study of History*, studied twenty one different civilizations that have passed through history's pages. He noted with certainty that others would follow.

In the final analysis, the academic and journalistic worlds mostly regard history as a record and explanation of past events. From a more practical perspective, history represents a sequence of building blocks—cultural, technological, military, and political—ready to be utilized and enhanced or maligned and perverted by the present. What that means is that all societies—whether advanced civilizations or preliterate tribal cultures—leave a legacy for succeeding generations to either embrace or disregard.

Recognizing the richness and fullness of history, the ReferencePoint Press Understanding World History series fosters an evaluation and interpretation of history and its influence on later generations. Each volume in the series approaches its subject chronologically and topically, with specific focus on nations, periods, or pivotal events. Primary and secondary source quotations are included, along with complete source notes and suggestions for further research.

Moreover, the series reflects the truism that the key to understanding the present frequently lies in the past. With that in mind, each series title concludes with a legacy chapter that highlights the bonds between past and present and, more important, demonstrates that world history is a continuum of peoples and ideas, sometimes hidden but there nonetheless, waiting to be discovered by those who choose to look.

Important Events of the Arab Spring Uprisings

1969
Muammar Gaddafi seizes power in Libya, becoming the first of the dictators whose authority would eventually be challenged during the Arab Spring.

January 13, 2011
The first protests against Libya's Gaddafi break out in the city of Benghazi as demonstrators march on abandoned construction sites to call attention to the poverty that engulfs their city.

1987
Dictator Zine al-Abidine Ben Ali seizes power in Tunisia; at first he promises democracy but soon turns his country into a police state and uses his office to loot the national treasury.

January 14, 2011
After the Tunisian army refuses to fire on protesters, Ben Ali resigns as president and flees to Saudi Arabia.

1980 / 2010 2011

1981
After the assassination of Anwar El Sadat, Hosni Mubarak ascends to the presidency of Egypt, beginning a thirty-year dictatorship in which he turns his country into a virtual police state.

June 2010
Activist Khaled Said is beaten to death by Egyptian police; images of the incident are uploaded onto the Internet, sparking protests.

December 17, 2010
After being abused by police, Tunisian fruit vendor Mohammed Bouazizi sets himself on fire, sparking mass demonstrations in Tunisia. This act is regarded as the official start of the Arab Spring.

January 25, 2011
The first mass protests occur in Cairo's Tahrir Square; apart from a few clashes with police, the demonstration is largely peaceful.

January 28, 2011
The Friday of Rage in Tahrir Square turns violent as police clash with protesters; eight people are killed in the melee.

February 17, 2011
A mass protest at the Al Manar plaza in Benghazi erupts into violence as Gaddafi's troops fire on demonstrators. Some protesters break into a military base and arm themselves, signaling the start of civil war in Libya.

March 17, 2011
The United Nations declares a no-fly zone over Libya, effectively providing rebels with Western military support.

June 2012
Egyptians elect Muslim Brotherhood member Mohamed Morsi as president; he promises to govern fairly.

July 2, 2013
After a year in office, Morsi is removed by the army after protestors return to Tahrir Square. Morsi's supporters stage violent street protests in which about one thousand people are killed.

October 20, 2011
Gaddafi is tracked down in the city of Sirte and executed by rebels.

2012   2013

August 21, 2013
According to US and international sources, Syrian troops launch a chemical weapons attack against civilians in the towns of Zamalka, Ein Tarma, and Jobar north of Damascus, killing nearly 1,500 people.

August 23, 2011
The Libyan capital of Tripoli falls into rebel hands, concluding the civil war and marking the end of the Gaddafi dictatorship.

March 20, 2011
Assad's police respond to demonstrators in the Syrian city of Dara'a by firing on the crowd, killing several people. Soon rebels arm themselves and civil war engulfs the country.

February 11, 2011
Under pressure from the Egyptian army and the Barack Obama administration, Mubarak resigns.

Introduction

The Defining Characteristics of the Arab Spring

In the Arab world there may have been no more ruthless dictator than Muammar Gaddafi. The junior army officer seized control of the North African nation of Libya in 1969, wresting power from an aging king. Gaddafi soon threw his enemies in prison, shut down unfriendly newspapers, installed his lackeys in key army posts, and kicked the American military out of a US Air Force base on the country's Mediterranean coast.

By the 2000 decade Gaddafi had also turned into an international pariah. He was alleged to have sponsored acts of terrorism—most notably the 1988 bombing of Pan American flight 103 over Lockerbie, Scotland, in which 280 people died. His brutality could also be directed at his own people: In 1996 Gaddafi ordered the massacre of as many as fourteen hundred inmates at Abu Salim prison in the Libyan capital of Tripoli, where the dictator jailed many of his political critics. Inmates had rioted in response to inhumane conditions at the prison, and Gaddafi responded by ordering a brutal crackdown.

The families of the massacred inmates wanted justice, so they turned to Fathi Terbil, a young Libyan lawyer and human rights activist. Given the iron grip Gaddafi held over his country and its courts, Terbil found himself virtually powerless to seek justice for the families he represented. For years Terbil demanded that the Libyan government reveal the truth about what happened at Abu Salim. Meanwhile, in

2010 Terbil and other activists started planning a public demonstration against Gaddafi. They intended to call the protest the Day of Anger.

By early 2011 the mood in Libya was reaching a boiling point. Gaddafi was well aware of the plans for the public demonstration—an unprecedented challenge to his authority. When Terbil filed a lawsuit against the regime, charging Libyan officials with complicity in the massacre, Gaddafi could endure these challenges no longer. On February 15, 2011, he ordered the arrest of Terbil.

Facebook, Twitter, and Al Jazeera

The young activist's arrest touched off a public demonstration in the streets of the Libyan city of Benghazi, a hotbed of dissent in the country. As many as two thousand people gathered in the city's streets, where they called for the release of Terbil and the ouster of Gaddafi. Leaders of the protest made use of the Internet and social media to spread news about the protest. Gaddafi controlled the Libyan press, but he had no power over Facebook, Twitter, and other social media forums; therefore, he was powerless to put down the demonstration before it started.

By the time the demonstration erupted in Benghazi, such scenes had become common throughout the Arab world. Libya was not the only Arab nation that had been ruled for decades by brutal dictators—the people of Egypt, Tunisia, Syria, Yemen, and other countries of the Middle East and North Africa had been similarly repressed. All those countries and others exploded in late 2010 and early 2011 in popular uprisings during an era known as the Arab Spring. Also known as the Arab Awakening, it was a time when citizens of the Arab states—many of them young—demanded the rights and opportunities common in Western democracies. Says Marc Lynch, a foreign policy advisor to President Barack Obama, "This was a generational change. This rising generation of young people had spent their formative years on the Internet, plotting their next protest rather than hiding from politics. Most could not even conceive of the world of the 1970s and 1980s when authoritarian regimes dominated every aspect of public life."[1]

Countries of the Arab Spring

Starting in December 2010, a wave of protest and upheaval spread across the Arab world. Leaders were toppled in Egypt, Tunisia, and Libya; violent unrest continued in Syria and elsewhere. Some countries, like Morocco and Jordan, were able to introduce reforms to find an uneasy peace.

Regime changed
Ongoing protests and violence
Major protests contained
Regime change and ongoing strife

Source: CBC News, "Where the Arab Protests Still Rage," February 6, 2013. www.cbc.ca.

As in Libya, the protests against entrenched dictators across the Arab world found traction on social media, where activists were able to plan demonstrations, rally supporters, and disseminate news. Another important factor in the popular uprisings of 2011 was the influence of Al Jazeera, the satellite TV news network based in Qatar. At the time, Al Jazeera was one of the few media outlets in the Arab world not controlled by a dictator. Launched in 1996, Al Jazeera is similar to the twenty-four-hour cable TV news networks in America. It features uncensored news as well as commentaries by political pundits and other advocates who supported the uprisings and therefore gave the protests legitimacy among the station's viewers. Says Ali Hashem, a former Al Jazeera correspondent:

> In the Arab countries, where people are used to listening on a daily basis to speeches by their leaders or members of ruling families, the new channel introduced counter-fire talk shows and documentaries from hotspots with an emphasis on controversial issues. For the first time, people saw opposition figures from around the Arab world saying in Arabic what they had only dared to say before on western channels in English or French.[2]

The Protests Turn Violent

The protest in Benghazi—as well as those in Cairo, Egypt; Sidi Bouzid, Tunisia; Manama, Bahrain; Sana'a, Yemen; and other cities in the Arab world—all started out peacefully, but most invariably mushroomed into violent confrontations between demonstrators and police or military units. Within hours of Terbil's arrest, citizens in Benghazi staged the Day of Anger. Most of the demonstrators, who were alerted to the protest by Facebook posts, marched on government offices and demanded the release of Terbil—who was ultimately set free by Libyan authorities. Soon, though, the Benghazi demonstration grew angry as protesters hurled rocks at government buildings and set nearby cars on fire. Police moved in and attempted to disperse the crowd, firing rubber bullets at the protesters and also spraying them with fire hoses.

But then the scene erupted in gunfire as Gaddafi's soldiers fired into the crowd, killing and wounding many protesters. Such efforts to quell the antigovernment protests would be repeated in other cities, but they would largely fail. By standing up against some of the world's most ruthless dictators, the activists of the Arab Spring showed remarkable courage as well as resiliency in their refusals to back down. Moreover, many of the protesters were women who found empowerment by demanding their rights. For centuries women have generally been regarded as second-class citizens in many Arab countries. Their status stems from interpretations by conservative clerics of the Koran—the Islamic holy book. These clerics often wield considerable influence in Arab countries.

Says Natana J. Delong-Bas, a professor of theology at Boston College:

> The Arab Spring introduced us to the strength and determination of the many Arab women who took to the streets and the Internet to call for change in their governments and societies. Gone were the stereotypes of oppression and passivity. In their place were voices and faces of hope, courage and indomitable spirit, calling for regime change and new, inclusive governments that would finally give women their rights and places in new societies free from corruption.[3]

Ripple Effect

Facing such overwhelming hostility toward their continued rule, some of the Arab dictators eventually backed down to the will of their peoples. They resigned and fled their countries. Some were arrested by the new governments and charged with human rights abuses. But some Arab leaders dug in, and in those cases armed civil war erupted. The country that has suffered the most devastating civil war is Syria, where longtime dictator Bashar al-Assad has refused to leave office. By late 2013 more than one hundred thousand Syrians had died in the civil war and millions had fled their homes, most taking refuge in neighboring Arab states. And on August 21, 2013, reports surfaced that Assad's military had launched chemical weapons on rebel positions near Damascus, killing some 1,500 civilians.

The unrest in Syria as well as other countries has had a ripple effect that has caused tensions elsewhere in the world. Russia, for example, has supported the Assad regime, supplying arms to the dictator, while the United States and other Western nations have endorsed the rebel cause but otherwise provided little support outside of humanitarian aid. In

Yemen a dictator has been ousted, but the new government has failed to maintain a vigilant guard against terrorists, and now portions of the country are regarded as safe havens for the extremist group al Qaeda.

Therefore, the Arab Spring has helped complicate an already complicated region of the world. Indeed, by the end of 2013 none of the countries that experienced upheaval during the Arab Spring could be said to be on firm democratic footings. They were either engaged in bloody civil war, as in the case of Syria, or, as in Tunisia and Egypt, attempting to make successes out of shaky democracies. But there is no question the Arab Spring has forever changed the Middle East and North Africa as young people have demanded their rights and access to the opportunities that would be available to them in free societies.

Chapter 1

What Conditions Led to the Arab Spring?

In ancient times the Middle East and North Africa were among the most advanced regions of the globe. The Egyptians built the pyramids and other archaeological wonders. In the city-state of Babylon, a region found in modern-day Iraq, a king named Hammurabi authored the first body of laws in which the rule of law was not applied arbitrarily but instead equally to all his subjects. (Many centuries later the framers of the US Constitution would find inspiration in the Code of Hammurabi.) In North Africa by the second century BCE the Carthaginians forged an advanced civilization and built one of the most powerful militaries on Earth.

But eventually these lands were conquered by the Romans and other European powers, and the people of the Middle East and North Africa found themselves reduced to poverty and illiteracy, squeezed into overpopulated and dirty cities, or living nomadic lives in the deserts. National borders held little meaning for most of the peoples of the ancient Arab world; instead, they looked to tribal leaders, or potentates, for guidance and protection. In the meantime the Arabs became a deeply religious people. Starting in the seventh century CE, the Arab peoples largely embraced the teachings of the Prophet Muhammad, who is said to have been commanded by God—known in the Islamic world as Allah—to repeat his words. Those words were soon rendered into written form in the Koran, the laws that guide the Islamic people.

Over the centuries, the Arab world grew into a largely diverse and dissimilar group of peoples. As the modern world emerged from medieval times, new discoveries and advancements were made in the sciences, arts, and literature. These advancements were mostly found in Europe and the New World, while the Arab world was largely left behind. Says author Milton Viorst, "The ailment of the Arabs, in an era when nationalism served as a channel to the modern world, was that their nationalistic roots had long since withered. . . . The Arabs shared a language, a way of life strongly shaped by Islam, and a range of historical experiences. But these elements had not sufficed to create a sense of nationhood."[4]

Promise of Self-Government

Stepping into this void to rule over the Arab peoples was the Ottoman Empire, centered in Turkey. The Ottomans conquered the Arab world in the sixteenth century, and for nearly four hundred years the Ottomans ruled over a domain that stretched from their capital in Constantinople to the Middle Eastern and North African capitals of Cairo in Egypt, Damascus in Syria, Baghdad in Iraq, Beirut in Lebanon, Tunis in Tunisia, and hundreds of other regions of the Arab world.

At no time during their long servitude under the Ottomans could the Arabs hope for self-rule, but when the world erupted into World War I in 1914, the Middle East and North Africa represented important fronts in the conflict. The Ottoman Turks joined the war on the side of Germany. The British engaged the Turks in the Middle East and North Africa and were aided in their campaign by Arab tribes who joined forces with the British when they were promised self-rule following the war.

The Arabs proved themselves brave and relentless guerilla fighters. To help lead what was soon known as the Great Arab Revolt, the British dispatched a junior officer named T.E. Lawrence, a swashbuckling adventurer who taught the Arabs modern tactics and equipped them with explosives to bury beneath railroad tracks that spanned the desert sands. When a Turkish troop or armaments train rode over one of these mines, it would explode. Lawrence and the Arabs blew up dozens of trains in this fashion over the course of the war. In describing one attack, Lawrence wrote, "A locomotive . . . had come up from Hedia [Morocco], and had exploded the mine fore and aft of its wheels. This was everything we had hoped, and we rode back to . . . camp on a morning of perfect springtime. . . . Mines were the best weapon yet discovered to make the regular working of their trains costly and uncertain for our Turkish enemy."[5]

But after the defeat of the Turks and Germans, promises of self-rule were soon forgotten as Great Britain as well as France sought to control most of the Middle Eastern and North African states as colonies. In 1921 Winston Churchill, then Great Britain's colonial secretary, agreed to provide an Arab royal family—the Hashemites, who are believed to be direct descendants of the Prophet Muhammad—with authority over a territory that today is the nation of Jordan. But for most of the rest

Anglo-Arab troops enter the Syrian city of Damascus in 1918 during the Great Arab Revolt. British promises of self-rule for their Arab allies did not materialize.

of the Middle East and North Africa, the European powers intended to remain firmly in control. "The [British] Cabinet raised the Arabs to fight for us by definite promises of self-government afterwards," Lawrence wrote after the war. "In our two years' partnership under fire [the Arabs] grew accustomed to believing me and to think my Government, like myself, sincere. In this hope they performed some fine things, but, of course, instead of being proud of what we did together, I was continually and bitterly ashamed."[6]

Leadership Struggles

By World War II (1939–1945), these states were still under the control of powerful European nations that refused to let most of the Arab world pursue self-rule. Libya, for example, was invaded by Italian Fascists under Benito Mussolini in the 1920s. Throughout the 1920s and 1930s, the French remained in control of Syria. The British granted the Egyptians nominal control of their own country, but British troops remained and the British government made it clear it would intervene in Egyptian affairs if British trade through the Suez Canal was threatened.

When World War II erupted, the Middle East and North Africa once again represented key strategic regions in the conflict. When the Allies drove the Italians and Germans out of North Africa in 1943, it all but spelled the end for Mussolini. The Allies soon launched an attack on Italy, crossing the Mediterranean Sea for an invasion that quickly knocked Italy out of the war. To invade Italy, Allied troops launched convoys from Tunisia, Algeria, and Libya.

Following World War II and the establishment of the United Nations, the states of the Middle East and North Africa were finally granted self-rule. Instead of settling in to stable democracies, though, most of the new Arab states struggled to find effective leaders who enjoyed the support of the people they represented as well as that of the key blocs of power within their countries—in most cases, the military. For example, between 1954 and 1970 the leadership of Syria changed seventeen times—in almost every case the president was toppled during military coups.

Iraq emerged from the war as a monarchy with a Hashemite, King Faisal, installed on the throne. But Faisal was overthrown in a military coup in 1958; an Iraqi general named Karim Kassem assumed power. He was assassinated five years later in a military coup. Another coup followed in 1968. By the late 1970s the president of Iraq was Ahmed Hassan al-Bakr. However, the real power in Iraq was held by the Iraqi vice president, Saddam Hussein; in 1979 Saddam forced al-Bakr to retire and assumed control of Iraq. Saddam would emerge as one of the Middle East's most ruthless dictators, oppressing his people while harboring few qualms about waging war against his neighbors.

Pan-Arab Unity

Perhaps the most stable leader to emerge during this era was Gamal Abdel Nasser of Egypt. In the aftermath of World War II, Egypt was led by King Farouk, whose family had ruled Egypt during the first half of the nineteenth century. In 1952 a group of army officers carried out a coup against Farouk and deposed the king. Emerging as the leader from this group of officers was Nasser, who assumed dictatorial powers and would, in fact, remain in power until his death in 1971.

Nasser saw his mission as more than just leading Egypt. He envisioned a "pan-Arab" community, meaning all Arabs would regard themselves not as Egyptians, Jordanians, Tunisians, and Libyans, but as members of a single Arab society. Nasser would never live to see his dream fulfilled: squabbling among Arab nations and internal problems within those countries would largely defeat his efforts to build pan-Arab unity.

Moreover, the United States and the Soviet Union were major players—often covertly—in the affairs of the Arab nations. Both of the superpowers sought influence in the region and were anxious to cement ties with their allies while undermining their enemies. The Soviets, for example, allied with the Egyptians and supplied Nasser with arms. The Saudis, led by a royal family, allied with the Americans, who were and still are major consumers of the country's vast oil reserves.

During the 1950s Nasser sponsored Radio Cairo, a radio station that broadcast throughout the entire Arab world, urging Arabs to join

Who Are the Hashemites?

The official name of the nation of Jordan is the Hashemite Kingdom of Jordan. Since establishment of the nation following World War I, Jordan has always been led by a Hashemite monarch.

The Hashemites trace their roots to Hashem, great-grandfather of the Prophet Muhammad, who lived in the seventh century CE. For centuries, Hashemite kings ruled over regions of the Middle East, including a portion of what is now Saudi Arabia. But starting in 1517, after conquest by the Ottomans, the Hashemites held little power.

Following the fall of the Ottomans, a Hashemite king, Abdullah, assumed the throne of Jordan while his brother, Faisal, ruled Syria and later Iraq. In 1958 Faisal was overthrown by the military in Iraq. In Jordan, Abdullah was killed by an assassin in 1951.

Despite this history of falling victim to violence, the Hashemites have managed to hold on to power in Jordan. After his death, Abdullah was succeeded by his son Talal, who ruled briefly but was removed from power when it became evident he suffered from mental illness. Talal was succeeded by a brother, Hussein, who ruled until his death in 1999. Since the death of King Hussein, his son Abdullah has reigned in Jordan.

forces under Egyptian leadership. To counter the effectiveness of Radio Cairo, the CIA covertly established its own Arab-language radio station, headquartered in Syria. The CIA's broadcasts attacked Nasser and warned Arab listeners of the dangers of allying with the Soviets. In the Middle East of the 1950s, this type of meddling by the superpowers was common.

War with Israel

Meanwhile, Nasser's efforts to achieve pan-Arab unity often fell short or were undone by his own deviousness. In 1956 Nasser and the leaders of Yemen and Saudi Arabia signed the Jedda Pact. Designed as a mutual protection agreement, the pact committed each of the signees to protect one another in the event of foreign attack. Nasser's true desire, though, was to bring the entire Arabian Peninsula under Egyptian authority. In 1962 he sponsored a coup in Yemen that soon turned into a civil war. Nasser sent forty thousand troops to Yemen, where they found themselves bogged down in the inhospitable mountainous country for five years until the Egyptians finally left in defeat. Nasser made another ill-fated attempt to forge pan-Arab unity in 1958 when he convinced the Syrians to form a political union, known as the United Arab Republic. The republic lasted a mere three years, dissolving when Nasser refused to share power with Syrian leaders.

But the most devastating blow to pan-Arab unity occurred in 1967 when Nasser as well as his allies in Syria and Jordan prepared to attack Israel. Not waiting for the attack to start, the Israelis launched a preemptive strike on air bases in Egypt and troop positions in Jordan and Syria. The three Arab armies proved themselves inept combatants; it was all over in six days—hence, the name for the conflict: the Six-Day War. As a result of the war, Israel seized huge swaths of land in Egypt, Jordan, and Syria to act as buffer zones against future attacks. In the wake of the war, the Jordanians found themselves housing tens of thousands of displaced Palestinian Arabs who fled the West Bank, an area across the Jordan River seized by Israel during the war. Some of these Palestinians dedicated themselves to terrorism in their cause to regain lost territory and establish a homeland. Jordan's King Hussein ruthlessly kicked them all out of his country, thereby turning his back on pan-Arab unity in the interest of pursuing peaceful relations with neighboring Israel.

After Nasser's death, he was succeeded by Anwar El Sadat, who had been one of the army officers who helped overthrow Farouk. After another unsuccessful war with Israel in 1973, Sadat signed a peace treaty with Egypt's longtime enemy, again dealing a blow to pan-Arab unity.

Despite his moderate policies, Sadat, too, served largely as a dictator and was assassinated in 1981 by Islamic fundamentalists. He was succeeded by vice president Hosni Mubarak, who exerted ruthless control over virtually every aspect of life in Egypt. Mubarak all but outlawed the Muslim Brotherhood, a group of Islamic fundamentalists who seek to rule Egypt and other Arab nations under the dictates of Islamic law. Brotherhood members, as well as other dissidents, were routinely jailed. Such policies were not limited to Egypt: by the 1980s despotic rule was the way of life in most Arab countries. Says Marc Lynch, "Arab regimes routinely resorted to brutal violence to crush their domestic opponents."[7]

The Persian Gulf War

In addition to crushing dissent in their own countries, these dictators have occasionally trained envious eyes on their neighbors. In 1990 Saddam Hussein sent his troops over the border to attack neighboring Kuwait to resolve a dispute over rights to oil fields. As Saddam's troops occupied Kuwait, the United States organized an international military coalition to drive the Iraqis out of Kuwait. The brief Persian Gulf War resulted in a humiliating defeat for the Iraqis.

The war represented another blow to pan-Arab unity because the Arab states were forced to choose sides. Jordan, Yemen, and Sudan stayed loyal to Iraq, although all three states stopped short of supplying troops or other military aid to Saddam. On the other hand, fearing that an Iraqi victory over Kuwait would empower Saddam to launch new attacks, the Gulf states—chiefly Saudi Arabia—allied with the United States and other members of the coalition.

The war caused many Islamic militants to seethe because the Saudis permitted their country to be used as a military staging base for the air attacks on Iraq. Many fundamentalist Muslims consider Saudi land holy and regarded its use by Western armies as sacrilegious. Among these fundamentalists was a wealthy Saudi, Osama bin Laden, who organized a terrorist group known as al Qaeda, or "the Base." Al Qaeda is responsible for a number of terrorist attacks—most notably the 2001

The CIA Meddling in Iran

An example of how the superpowers meddled in the Middle East can be found in Iran, which in 1951 took a major step toward democracy with the election of Mohammad Mosaddegh as prime minister. Soon after his election, Mosaddegh nationalized his country's oil industry and seized control of oil wells from Western-based private corporations, most of which were headquartered in Great Britain.

To help the British regain control of their assets, the CIA organized a coup against Mosaddegh. In his place the CIA installed a member of Iranian royalty, Shah Mohammad Reza Pahlavi, who ruled as a dictator but was nevertheless friendly to Western oil companies.

The shah was overthrown in 1979 by Islamic extremists, who have ruled with dictatorial control. The Green Revolution of 2009 was the first time dissidents challenged Iran's ruling mullahs, the Islamic clergy leaders. Hamid Dabashi, professor of Iranian Studies at Columbia University, argues that under Mosaddegh Iran may have maintained a democratic course, but the coup gave the Islamists the resolve to eventually wrest power from the shah. He says, "To this day, the coup remains a gushing wound—a trauma that has benighted much of modern Iranian political culture and been widely abused by the [mullahs] to justify [their] absolutist reign of terror."

Hamid Dabashi, "Mosaddegh and the Legacy of Non-aligned Movement," Al Jazeera, August 26, 2012. www.aljazeera.com.

attacks on the World Trade Center in New York City and the Pentagon in Washington, DC. When the United States organized the invasion of Iraq in 2003, it was due in part to President George W. Bush's belief that Saddam had aided al Qaeda.

Wary Eye on the Arab World

During the Iraq War and the aftermath of the 2001 terrorist attacks, the Arab nations of the Middle East and North Africa found themselves again choosing up sides—some siding with the Americans and their allies, some remaining loyal to a pan-Arab cause. Egypt, for example, remained a staunch ally of America during this era and is known to have taken suspected al Qaeda members into custody and subjected them to torture in order to produce intelligence exposing al Qaeda's plans.

Meanwhile, more than a decade after the invasion of Iraq, America and other Western nations have kept a close and wary eye on the Arab world, believing the nations of the Middle East and North Africa serve as breeding grounds for religious extremists and terrorists. And, thanks to their involvement in Arab affairs, foreigners have had a measure of influence over the politics and policies in the Arab world. For example, since the Persian Gulf War, the US military has maintained bases in Kuwait. In 2013 the French military intervened to establish peace in the North African country of Mali after Islamic extremists overthrew the government in the former French colony. In many cases foreign powers have helped prop up dictators. Throughout the Mubarak era, the United States provided Egypt with $2 billion a year in foreign aid. Moreover, Mubarak and other Arab dictators were often supplied with arms. Says journalist Nick Turse, who writes on national security issues, "For decades, the U.S. has provided military aid, facilitated the sale of weaponry, and transferred vast quantities of arms to a host of Middle Eastern despots."[8]

The Green Revolution

During the 1990s and the 2000 decade, occasional protests erupted against the Arab dictators. Most lacked widespread public support and were put down quickly by police, but nevertheless these protests offered a glimpse of the rowdy demonstrations that would arrive in 2010 and 2011. In Egypt, for example, the Kefaya movement (*kefaya* is an Arabic word meaning "enough") staged demonstrations in 2004 and 2005. Kefaya demonstrated in support of the displaced Palestinian people, in opposition to the American invasion of Iraq, and in opposition to Mubarak's plans to appoint his son, Gamal, as his successor. Although they were an early and important challenge to the power of Mubarak's rule, the Kefaya demonstrations were rarely attended by more than a few hundred protesters.

Perhaps the most significant precursor to the Arab Spring occurred in Iran—a Middle Eastern country that is not populated by Arabs. (Although virtually surrounded by Arab nations, Iranians are largely ethnic Persians, and Farsi—not Arabic—is the native language.) In 1979 the American-backed monarch of Iran, Shah Mohammad Reza Pahlavi, was driven from power in a revolution led by a fundamentalist Islamic movement under Ayatollah Ruhollah Khomeini. Over the past three decades, the mullahs—Islamic clergy leaders—in charge of the country have established a repressive oligarchy. Opponents of the regime are imprisoned, women are granted few rights, and elections are regarded as shams. Moreover, the regime has pursued an anti-American foreign policy and is believed to be developing nuclear weapons. In response, America and most European nations have imposed a tight economic boycott over Iran, cutting off trade with the country. This boycott has led to harsh living conditions in Iran, since the country, although oil rich, is unable to obtain many basic consumer goods.

In 2009 tens of thousands of demonstrators took to the streets of Tehran, the Iranian capital, to protest the sham election of President Mahmoud Ahmadinejad. Since the Iranian media is tightly controlled by the mullahs, the protest leaders turned to Facebook, Twitter, and other social media to organize public demonstrations. The demonstrations became known as the Green Revolution. The mullahs acted decisively, sending in police and paramilitary thugs to break up the protesting crowds. Dozens of peaceful protesters were beaten and pepper sprayed, but in one instance gunfire erupted and resulted in the death of a young woman, Neda Agha-Soltan—whose death at the hands of authorities was captured on video and uploaded to YouTube. In an Internet posting, her fiancé, Caspian Makan, wrote, "She wanted freedom, freedom for everybody."[9]

Tens of thousands of Iranian citizens march through the streets of Tehran to protest the 2009 presidential election victory of Mahmoud Ahmadinejad. Iran's Green Revolution inspired and empowered oppressed people throughout the Middle East.

Although unsuccessful, the Green Revolution proved the oppressed people of the Middle East could make their voices heard, and these voices would empower others to stand up for their rights as well. As the dictators of the Arab world were soon to learn, many of these uprisings would not be as easily suppressed.

Chapter 2

Tunisia's Jasmine Revolution

In the years before dictator Zine al-Abidine Ben Ali rose to power in 1987, Tunisia was, at least for a brief time, a model of progressive government and culture in the Arab world. Ben Ali's predecessor, Habib Bourguiba, had been able to turn the dusty North African country into a bustling society where human rights were emphasized. In 1956, soon after Tunisia was granted its independence from France, Bourguiba was elected president in a democratic process.

Moreover, the Tunisian parliament, known as the Chamber of Deputies, adopted the most progressive law in the Arab world protecting the rights of women: the Statute of Women and the Family. The law banned polygamy and established definite procedures for divorce. Under the new law a man could no longer rid himself of his wife by simply renouncing their marriage—a common practice in the Arab world. Under Tunisian law, spouses had to follow legal procedures for divorce based on laws found on the books in western European nations. It was an important protection for women, who could no longer be cast out of their homes on the whims of their husbands.

Nevertheless, although Bourguiba promoted many reforms, he soon sought wide-ranging and dictatorial powers. By the early 1960s Tunisia was a one-party state with Bourguiba's party, eventually known as the Democratic Constitutional Rally (RCD), in firm control of the government. By then Bourguiba had assumed a dictator's grip over his nation's government. In fact, in 1974 Bourguiba had himself declared president for life.

Fierce Crackdown

As long as the country prospered, Tunisians tolerated Bourguiba's dictatorial conduct, but by 1984 food shortages led to rioting in the streets. The government responded with a fierce crackdown, imprisoning hundreds of demonstrators. In 1987, believing he needed to wield an even heavier hand to control his unruly citizens, Bourguiba appointed Ben Ali, a tough army general, as prime minister. By now the Tunisian government was in disarray, the population unhappy, and the economy in shambles.

As for Bourguiba, his behavior was highly erratic. He ordered the arrests of about six thousand Tunisians whom he regarded as political enemies. At that point, Ben Ali pressed for the president's removal: he appointed a panel of doctors, who declared that the president suffered from dementia. Under the terms of the Tunisian constitution, Ben Ali had Bourguiba removed from office on medical grounds.

Ben Ali also assumed the presidency and declared that he would return democracy to Tunisians. "The era we live in can no longer stand for a president for life, nor an automatic succession to the head of the state from which the people [find themselves] excluded,"[10] the new president said soon after taking office.

Controlling Elections

Tunisians found those words inspiring. Had Ben Ali kept his promise to reform Tunisia, his country may have once again stood out as a model of progressive culture in the Arab world. Instead, Ben Ali took a much different path—a path that would eventually light the fuse that sparked the Arab Spring.

At first, it appeared as though Ben Ali intended to make reforms. He freed the political prisoners and permitted establishment of opposition political parties. These reforms turned out to be hollow: The Tunisian constitution drafted under Bourguiba provided little power to political opponents, and Ben Ali showed no interest in reforming the system. In the parliamentary elections of 1989, the first elections held during Ben Ali's tenure as president, opposition parties won no seats in the Chamber of Deputies.

Early in his presidency Ben Ali (pictured here in 2009) promised democracy for Tunisia. Instead he became increasingly authoritarian, a path that led eventually to the revolution that sparked the Arab Spring.

In subsequent elections the RCD would easily maintain its control over the Tunisian government. In the 2004 presidential election, for example, Ben Ali won reelection with 99.9 percent of the vote. Ben Ali was able to maintain such majorities by making sure most opposition candidates were kicked off the ballot—or, if he did permit opposing candidates to run for president, he simply made sure their votes were not counted.

Silencing Dissent, Looting the Treasury

These overwhelming victories by Ben Ali and his hand-picked cronies in the Chamber of Deputies reflected the fact that in the years since Bourguiba had been removed from power, nothing in Tunisia had really changed. Political dissent in Tunisia was still not tolerated. "Here, it's like in all Arab countries: We don't criticize the leader and we don't have the right to approach politics,"[11] a fifty-four-year-old Tunisian named Moncef told a Western journalist in 2004. Out of fear of reprisal by the government, Moncef refused to give his last name to the reporter—a typical response by Tunisians interviewed by Western news media.

Indeed, by the 2000 decade Ben Ali's dictatorial control was at its peak. He had outlawed an-Nahda, the country's main Islamist party, and thrown its leaders in prison. Ben Ali, as well as dictators through-out the Arab world, found himself with much to fear from radical Islamists. They were prepared to resort to violence, and many would readily sacrifice their lives for their cause—and that cause was to rule their homelands under conservative interpretations of the Koran.

In addition to suppressing Islamist voices, Ben Ali also silenced other dissent largely by maintaining firm control over the Tunisian media. As Ben Ali celebrated twenty years in power, the Tunisian French-language newspaper *La Presse* proclaimed, "On this 20th an-niversary . . . Tunisians of all categories and ages are celebrating with extraordinary pride, the economic, political and social achievements initiated and promoted by President Ben Ali. . . . Our conviction [is confirmed] that Tunisia's development experience is a model to be followed."[12]

Over the years, as Ben Ali tightened his grip on the Tunisian gov-ernment, he came to regard the job of president as mainly a license to loot the national treasury. Ben Ali and his wife, Leila Trabelsi, were known to seize properties and businesses at will. They lived in lavish palaces—it was said the couple's daughter, Nisrene, kept a pet tiger. At one dinner party in Ben Ali's palace in Tunis, the capital city, American ambassador Robert Godec related that the dictator boasted he had the dessert flown in on a private jet especially for the party from the French resort city of Saint-Tropez—about 600 miles (966 km) across the Mediterranean Sea. Eventually, it was estimated by financial officials in the Tunisian government that Ben Ali's sys-temic looting of his country's treasury had helped him amass a per-sonal fortune of $18 billion.

The Fruit Vendor

For most of the Tunisian people, though, life was far less luxurious. When she visited Tunisia in 2010, American journalist Phyllis Meras found widespread poverty and little opportunity for people to improve their lives. Speaking with one Tunisian who begged not to be identified in the media out of fear of reprisal from Ben Ali's government, Meras was told: "There is poverty in Tunisia these days and it's hard to find jobs. My sister was able to find work for six months, but then she was let go. Life isn't easy for us. Some Tunisians are lucky enough to find work abroad. Sicily, after all, is only ninety miles away (the nearest point of Italian land), but we'd like to have work at home."[13] Moreover, throughout Tunisia Meras found a heavy police presence—making her believe Tunisia was essentially a police state because Ben Ali believed he needed to control his people with a heavy hand. "Sometimes . . . police would be blocking off streets, making me vaguely wonder how repressive the government might be,"[14] Meras observed.

That police presence would be felt by Mohammed Bouazizi, a street vendor in the central Tunisian city of Sidi Bouzid. Bouazizi scratched out a meager livelihood selling fruit from a street cart. As with most people of Sidi Bouzid, Bouazizi lived in virtual poverty. The town is little more than a dusty crossroads that lacks adequate housing, health care, and other necessities of modern life. Bouazizi was barely able to feed his family of eight with the money he earned selling fruit.

Bouazizi, just twenty-six, had endured abuse at the hands of Tunisian authorities—he did not have a license to sell fruit, and the police responded by seizing his cart several times. Finally, on December 17, 2010, he argued with a Tunisian policewoman who confiscated his cart again. Moreover, she spoke harshly of Bouazizi's dead father and slapped his face—grave insults in the Arab world. Later that day Bouazizi stood in front of the government headquarters in Sidi Bouzid, doused himself with paint thinner, and set himself on fire. Bouazizi died on January 4, 2011. "What kind of repression do you

In January 2011 Tunisians rally around a portrait of Mohammed Bouazizi, a produce vendor who set himself on fire after several run-ins with police. Bouazizi's desperate act led to a citizen uprising against Tunisia's repressive government.

imagine it takes for a young man to do this?" asked his sister, Leila. "A man who has to feed his family by buying goods on credit when they have no connections and no money for bribes, are humiliated and insulted and not allowed to live."[15]

Throughout the deeply religious Arab world, women are often accorded few rights. For example, the Koran, the Muslim holy book, gives husbands permission to strike their wives if they are disobedient. Says the Koran, "The righteous women are devoutly obedient. . . . As to those women on whose part ye fear disloyalty and ill-conduct, admonish them (first), (next) . . . beat them (lightly)."

Tunisian political leaders have opposed that attitude for nearly a century. In post–World War I Tunisia, which was under the rule of France, Tunisian leaders sought to build support for independence by promising all citizens—including women—equality under a Tunisian-ruled nation. By the time Tunisia won its independence from France in 1956, that philosophy had been embraced by the country's first president, Habib Bourguiba.

"In particular, Bourguiba was attentive to this message, something he passionately embraced and vigorously embodied in the constitutional apparatus of Tunisia's first republic over which he was the chief executive for thirty years," says Larbi Sadiki, a senior lecturer in Middle Eastern politics at the University of Exeter in Great Britain. "The end result was Bourguiba's 1956 [Statute of Women and the Family] which enshrined the principle of gender equality, which banned polygamy, amongst other laws."

1. Quoted in *Christian Science Monitor*, "What the Koran Says About Women," December 19, 2001. www.csmonitor.com.
2. Larbi Sadiki, "Tunisia: Women's Rights and the New Constitution," Al Jazeera, September 21, 2012. www.aljazeera.com.

The Jasmine Revolution

The harsh treatment of Bouazizi at the hands of the police was typical of life in Tunisia. Over the years, Ben Ali had given the police widespread powers to suppress dissent by abusing people, arresting them on trumped up charges, jailing them without trials, and subjecting them to torture.

As part of his campaign to suppress radical Islam, Ben Ali had many conservative Muslims seized off the streets. One such victim was Abdel Karim Harouni, who was arrested in 1988 as he emerged from a mosque after prayers in the town of La Marsa. Harouni was shoved into a car by plainclothes officers and taken to a police station, where he was accused of helping to organize an-Nahda. Harouni says the charge was untrue, but the police were eager to beat a confession out of him. "I was stripped . . . hung roast-chicken style from a bar between two tables and beaten very hard with lengths of cable,"[16] he told a reporter in 2011. Harouni spent almost sixteen years in a Tunisian prison. "The regime was afraid that if there was freedom, people would choose Islamists," says Harouni. "For that we paid a heavy price."[17]

Many Tunisians told similar stories. One such victim was Naoufel Meddeb, the owner of a paper and office supply business in Tunis. In 2001 he delivered a copier to the Tunisian Justice Ministry. Instead of paying him the price of 800,000 Tunisian dinars (about US $4,900) for the machine, a ministry official wrote "free of charge" on the invoice. When Meddeb protested, the official told him, "We give you a lot of business, and it's normal for merchants to throw in a few things for free."[18]

Meddeb refused to accept the loss of payment, and the following year he filed a lawsuit against the Tunisian government seeking to collect his money. Soon after filing the lawsuit, Meddeb found himself the victim of government harassment. He was audited and charged 1.6 million dinars (about US $9,800) in back taxes. His office was broken into and ransacked four times—incidents he blames on the police. When he met with a judge to try to reach an agreement with the government, he was suddenly arrested and accused of the trumped-up charge of trafficking in stolen goods. He spent most of the next five years in prison. "Prison woke me up," he said. "Prison told me how ignorant I was."[19]

And so when news of Bouazizi's ultimate act of protest surfaced, Tunisians like Meddeb and Harouni felt a special bond with the destitute fruit vendor and decided to speak up against the dictator and his corrupt government. Soon, Bouazizi's act of defiance would lead to an unprecedented uprising among ordinary Tunisians against Ben Ali's repressive government. To Tunisians, the uprising became known as the Jasmine Revolution—named for the aromatic flower sold by street vendors.

Cyberwarfare

Street demonstrations erupted in Sidi Bouzid on December 18, the day after Bouazizi set himself on fire. Ordinary citizens, many of them as destitute as Bouazizi, but many also of more prosperous means, joined the demonstrations. At first, news of the uprising was carried exclusively over social media. Photos as well as videos of the demonstrations were posted on Facebook, YouTube, and elsewhere on the Internet. Activists developed Twitter followings. Within days, though, the Qatar-based TV network Al Jazeera dispatched news crews to Tunisia to cover the demonstrations.

Social media as well as the news coverage by Al Jazeera would prove to be vitally important components in the Jasmine Revolution. While Tunisian newspapers and local radio and TV stations, which were under Ben Ali's control, ignored the demonstrations, the people of Tunisia turned to social media and Al Jazeera for news of the protests as well as photos and videos. Said Rochdi Horchani, a relative of Bouazizi, "We could protest for two years here, but without videos no one would take notice of us."[20] Cell phones were also put to use as protesters texted news and plans to one another. According to Horchani, protesters took to the streets with "a rock in one hand, a cellphone in the other."[21]

Ben Ali responded by trying to take down the Internet. In Sidi Bouzid electric power was suddenly cut off to the whole town—evidently with no purpose other than to ensure that computer and TV screens would remain dark. The Tunisian authorities then turned to phishing tactics: they are believed to have uncovered users' passwords to disrupt communications and spread phony news. To wipe out criticism of the government, websites were taken down. One victim of the phishing campaign was Sofiene Chourabi, a Tunisian who maintained a blog where he posted harsh criticisms of the Tunisian government. According to Chourabi, his Facebook account and Gmail address were temporarily taken over by imposters. "My personal account on Facebook, including around 4,200 friends, was exposed to a failed hacking attempt . . . but I quickly recovered it after an unidentified person had taken control of it,"[22] he told a reporter for Al Jazeera.

Appeal for Calm

Still, the uprising persisted. By the end of the month, protests and riots were under way in most Tunisian cities, finally culminating on December 28, 2010, with a mass protest staged in the streets of Tunis. The demonstrators called for human rights, jobs, and an end to corruption. Their call was not a plea to the government to enact new policies; rather, they demanded immediate and widespread change. The most common chant heard during the demonstrations was "*Dégage!*," French for "Get out!"[23]—a message clearly aimed at the president.

A Tunisian flag flutters as protesters demand change in a massive rally in February 2011. Through their efforts, Tunisian dictator Ben Ali was forced out of office.

With demonstrations rampant throughout Tunisia, Ben Ali responded to this challenge to his authority as Arab despots had typically reacted in the past—by sending in the police and the military to break up the demonstrations and ordering the arrests of leaders. By January 10, 2011, several of the movement's leaders had been jailed, including Hamada Ben Amor, a Tunisian rapper whose song "Mr. President, Your People Are Dying" was widely available online. Meanwhile, nearly 150 protesters were believed to have been killed by police and army units. Nevertheless, the protests continued, and thousands of activists refused to leave the streets.

Ben Ali appeared on TV and appealed for calm—to no avail. The demonstrations in the streets continued. Using social media, leaders of the protest movement called for a general strike on January 13—asking all workers to stay home from their jobs and instead take to the streets. The strike continued into January 14 when tens of thousands of protesters crowded onto Bourguiba Boulevard, the wide, tree-lined thoroughfare in downtown Tunis.

Ben Ali Flees Tunisia

By this time Ben Ali had few allies. He made one final appeal, this time to Army Chief of Staff Rachid Ammar, ordering him to crack down on the Bourguiba Boulevard protesters. But Ammar refused. He may not have believed his forces were up to the task: Ben Ali, aware that army officers had often engineered coups in the Arab world, had purposely kept the army small and ill equipped. It is possible that if the situation in Tunisian cities deteriorated into street battles, Ammar would not have believed his troops capable of containing the dissidents.

It is also likely, however, that Ammar put his country before his president. Some reports suggested Ammar told Ben Ali he would resign rather than order his troops to fire on Tunisians. Jacques Lanxade, a former French ambassador to Tunisia, said, "It's the army which walked out on Ben Ali when it refused—unlike the regime's police—to fire on the crowds."[24] Lanxade further suggested that it was Ammar who told Ben Ali that his presidency was at an end. Without the backing of the

The Plight of Mohammed Bouazizi

Mohammed Bouazizi's act of self-sacrifice helped ignite the Arab Spring, but those who knew him said he had no interest in politics and was dedicated only to providing for his family. Bouazizi had been supporting his family since the age of twelve, following the death of his father and a debilitating illness suffered by a stepfather. As Bouazizi pushed his fruit cart along the streets of Sidi Bouzid, he was constantly harassed by police who would help themselves to fruit, demand bribes, or confiscate his goods. On the day he set himself on fire, police confiscated fruit valued at about $225 from his cart. Says human rights activist Hernando de Soto:

> If committing suicide over the loss of $225 worth of goods and a regular location on the street for a fruit stand seems inconceivable to most people in the United States and Europe, Bouazizi's counterparts throughout Tunisia and . . . the rest of the Arab world understood immediately his desperation. In their eyes, Bouazizi had not been just the victim of corruption or even public humiliation, as horrible as they are; he had been deprived of the only thing that stood between him and starvation—the loss of his place in the only economy available to poor Arabs.

Hernando de Soto, "The Real Mohamed Bouazizi," *Foreign Policy*, December 16, 2011. www.foreignpolicy.com.

army, the dictator realized he had lost all authority in his country and was now helpless to salvage his regime.

On January 14, 2011, Ben Ali boarded a plane for Saudi Arabia, where the former dictator had been promised safe haven. The Saudis are led by a monarch, King Abdullah, who has long seen his nation's role as one of keeping peace throughout the Arab world. Under the terms of the Saudi constitution, Saudi Arabia "shall grant the right to political asylum when the public interest demands this."[25] In the king's view, it was in the interest of the Saudi government to maintain calm in the Arab world; the king reasoned that handing Ben Ali over to a court in Tunisia would have contributed to a tense situation in that country that could have spilled over into the rest of the Arab world.

By mid-2013 the former dictator and his wife were still living in Saudi Arabia, fighting efforts to bring them back to Tunisia. Soon after they fled Tunisia, Ben Ali and his wife were tried and convicted in absentia on charges of looting the national treasury as well as of human rights abuses. Each was sentenced to thirty-five years in prison. Even if Tunisia wins Ben Ali's extradition, the ex-president is unlikely to serve much of his term. After he fled Tunisia it was revealed Ben Ali was suffering from prostate cancer. He was also reported to have suffered a debilitating stroke in Saudi Arabia.

Ben Ali was the first of the Arab dictators ousted in what would soon become known as the Arab Spring. For the Arab peoples of North Africa and the Middle East, the Arab Spring marked an awakening by the tens of millions of oppressed people, few of whom had ever known true freedom during their lifetime.

Chapter 3 🌐

Eighteen Days That Changed Egypt

Egypt is by far the largest of the Arab nations: Some 80 million people live in the North African country. It is also one of the poorest. The major cities of Cairo and Alexandria lack employment opportunities for their very large populations of young people. Over the decades the infrastructure of the cities—the roads, bridges, parks, and other public places—have fallen into disrepair. And yet it was no secret that Hosni Mubarak and his cronies had made themselves wealthy, mostly by accepting bribes and looting the national treasury. By 2011 the widely read Algerian newspaper *Al Khabar* reported that Mubarak's personal wealth totaled $70 billion; his son and designated heir to the Egyptian presidency, Gamal Mubarak, was also a billionaire.

Mubarak was able to exert dictatorial control over Egypt by making his country into a virtual police state. By 2010 around 1.4 million Egyptians—or about one in every sixty Egyptians—were employed in some capacity by the police. Many were not above using violent tactics and torture to keep the restive population in line.

Mubarak created a police state under the powers of an Egyptian law adopted in the wake of the 1981 assassination of Anwar El Sadat: To quell similar uprisings against the government, the Egyptian police were given widespread authority to detain citizens indefinitely and extract confessions from arrestees through the use of torture. In the decades following Sadat's assassination, human rights groups suggested that as many as ten thousand Egyptians had been tossed into Mubarak's prisons—and most of them were likely to have died at the hands of the police.

At the same time Mubarak built up and empowered the police, he was careful to keep the army out of politics. He sought to isolate both the military leaders and rank-and-file troops from political involvement, knowing full well that in the Arab world, army officers were often behind political coups.

"We Are All Khaled Said"

As in Tunisia, the heavy-handed tactics of the police would help spark revolution. Six months before Mohammed Bouazizi set himself on fire to protest harsh police tactics in Tunisia, a similar incident occurred in Egypt. In June 2010 a young Egyptian political activist, Khaled Said, was dragged out of an Internet café in Alexandria and beaten to death by police.

Witnesses said two plainclothes police officers entered the café and immediately started punching and kicking the twenty-eight-year-old activist, a successful entrepreneur and the son of a wealthy family. Said's head was smashed against a staircase, then he was dragged out of the café and tossed into a car. Ten minutes later, the car returned and dumped the victim's dead body onto the street. Unknown to the plainclothes officers, their activities had been photographed on cell phones by numerous witnesses in the café. Many of the pictures posted on the Internet displayed Said's bruised and bloodied face. "Witness accounts and the photographs of Khaled Said's mangled face constitute strong evidence that plainclothes security officers beat him in a vicious and public manner," said Joseph Stork, the deputy Middle East and North Africa director for the international group Human Rights Watch. "All those involved should be speedily interrogated, and the prosecutor should fully investigate what caused the fractures and trauma clearly evident on his body."[26]

Activists reacted quickly, posting a Facebook page titled "We Are All Khaled Said" to call attention to the young man's death. Within

The Trial of Said's Killers

The two police officers charged in the death of Khaled Said were convicted on the charge of manslaughter—a lesser charge than murder that often suggests the victim's death was not caused intentionally. In October 2011, about nine months after Hosni Mubarak left office, the two police officers, Mahmoud Salah and Awad Ismaeil, were each sentenced to seven years in prison.

Dissidents whose activism led to the arrests of Salah and Ismaeil were outraged at the sentence, believing it too lenient—although Gamal Eid, a human rights lawyer, said that during Mubarak's regime any trial for police officers would have been unthinkable. Supporters of the two police officers also expressed outrage, charging that the two men were scapegoats. Even Ali Qassem, Said's uncle, said he believes higher-ranking police officials should have been held accountable for the death of his nephew. "I feel pity for the defendants, for these underdogs," said Qassem. "They are mere scapegoats."

Activist Wael Ghonim, who helped establish the "We Are All Khaled Said" page on Facebook, said the sentences for the two police officers should have been longer. "We have the right to be angry," he said. "But we are in battle, and the rights of Khaled and all Egyptians like him will be returned."

1. Quoted in Sarah Carr, "Khaled Said Lawyers Demand Murder Charges, Trial Adjourned to Sept. 25," *Daily News Egypt* (Dokki, Egypt), July 27, 2010. www.dailynewsegypt.com.
2. Quoted in Heba Afify, "Officers Get 7 Years for Killing That Helped Inspire Egypt's Revolt," *New York Times*, October 26, 2011, p. A-14.

days of Said's death, several thousand Egyptians took to the streets of Alexandria to demand justice. As they marched they chanted "Down with Mubarak!" At first, Egyptian authorities ignored the protests, but activists kept up the pressure. By early July 2010 the "We Are All

Khaled Said" Facebook page had drawn nearly two hundred thousand followers. When news of the case first surfaced, the Egyptian government denied that the plainclothes police officers had done anything wrong, but the constant pressure brought by the activists convinced government leaders to change course. That month, the Egyptian government announced that two police officers would be charged with manslaughter—a lesser charge than murder that often suggests the death was caused unintentionally. "Khaled Said has done a very important thing," said Negad al-Borai, a prominent Egyptian human rights lawyer. "He has brought attention to what normal people go through. Every battle has its victims."[27]

An Egyptian woman solemnly marks the second anniversary of the June 2010 death of political activist Khaled Said at the hands of Egyptian police. Said's death ignited public outrage over rampant police brutality under then-president Hosni Mubarak.

White T-Shirts

Although the death of Said did at first spark some street protests, tight control by police contained much of the dissent. Still, young activists maintained an Internet campaign and adopted the white T-shirt as a symbol of protest. By wearing white T-shirts, activists could show their solidarity without arousing the wrath of the police, who were on the lookout for anyone brazen enough to challenge Mubarak by wearing clothes carrying incendiary messages.

This quiet campaign did have an effect. In late November and early December 2010, the Egyptian government staged parliamentary elections. Over the course of Mubarak's rule, such elections were regarded as nothing less than farcical—the dictator's hand-picked candidates were invariably easy winners, thanks to fraudulent vote counting. This time was no different: Mubarak's party, the National Democratic Party, won a sweeping victory, capturing a majority of the seats. Stork, the Human Rights Watch official, called the elections a sham. "The total lack of transparency about these elections puts the burden on Egyptian authorities to show others how these elections were not fatally compromised,"[28] Stork declared.

Dissidents also feared that by engineering a sweep of the 2010 election, Mubarak was sending a message about his intentions for the 2011 election, in which he was expected to run for another term as president. Clearly, dissidents expected Mubarak to run for another term, win easily, and then begin grooming his son Gamal to step into the presidency at some point. At the time of the 2010 election, Hosni Mubarak was eighty-two years old.

Fearing a Gamal Mubarak Presidency

In Egypt activists for change believed they had much to fear from an ascension to the presidency by Gamal Mubarak. Although Gamal's supporters pointed out that as a former banker, the younger Mubarak would bring an expertise to reviving the stagnant Egyptian economy, dissidents remained wary of the prospect of his presidency. They pointed out that the elder Mubarak and the insiders in his government would not be preparing Gamal for the presidency if the son had not promised to maintain the type of dictatorial control that Egyptians had lived under since the days of Gamal Abdel Nasser. Under Gamal Mubarak, they suggested, there would be no political reform and certainly no improvement in Egypt's poor record on observing human rights.

Moreover, many dissidents suggested Gamal's ascension to the presidency would remove all doubt among Egyptians and others that Egypt was anything but a dictatorship—and that democracy was simply not a way of life in the nation. After all, Saudi Arabia, Jordan, and other Arab states maintained monarchies, and rule was guaranteed under law and tradition to members of the royal families. But Egyptians had gotten rid of their monarchy in 1952. Permitting Gamal to ascend to the presidency would suggest that the Mubarak family had somehow claimed a monarchical right to rule. Said Alaa Al-Aswany, an Egyptian writer and founding member of the Kefaya movement:

> At the core of [Gamal Mubarak's ascension to the presidency] lies a single notion: that Egypt can be inherited like a farm or a piece of real estate. This notion, apart from the profound contempt it implies towards the Egyptian people, runs against the grain of the future, eliminates all hope Egyptians may have for justice and freedom and closes the door on any democratic reform for years to come. The moment Egypt is now going through is decisive: it leaves no room for compromise or vacillation. Egyptians will no longer be able to sit on the fence or try to please all sides. It is the moment of truth when we have to choose: either we assert our rights as respected citizens or we agree to be treated as slaves which the son can inherit from his father.[29]

As with the killing of Said, the 2010 election did prompt some street protests throughout Egypt, but they were quickly quelled by police. Nevertheless, activists did find one positive message in the election: Some 65 percent of Egyptian voters stayed home. To activists, it meant that most Egyptians knew full well their votes would be meaningless. Dissidents believed strongly now that the majority of Egyptians would support regime change.

"Day of Revolution"

The votes in the 2010 election were counted on December 5. Twelve days later Bouazizi set himself on fire. As the Tunisian people swarmed onto the streets of Tunis and other cities to protest the government of Zine al-Abidine Ben Ali, the Egyptian people followed the events closely on Al Jazeera as well as on social media.

Young Egyptian activists knew their opportunity was at hand to oust the Mubarak government. Among their leaders were Wael Ghonim, a Middle East–based employee of Google, and youth activists Abdul Rahman Mansour and Ahmed Saleh. The three activists were the organizers behind the "We Are All Khaled Said" Facebook page; now they turned their attention to organizing a public demonstration. Using social media, they called on activists to gather in Cairo's Tahrir Square on January 25, 2011. In Alexandria activists were urged to march on the Corniche, the city's massive waterfront district.

Again, Ghonim, Mansour, and Saleh turned to social media to plan the demonstrations in Tahrir Square and the Corniche. They established a Facebook page titled "Day of Revolution," and within a few days more than ninety thousand people had signed up as followers. The "Day of Revolution" page urged Egyptians to participate in the demonstrations to protest against Mubarak's dictatorial rule as well as to call attention to the poverty, corruption, torture, and unemployment that had afflicted the Egyptian people throughout his regime. "There are a lot of things wrong with this country," Ramy Rafat, a twenty-five-year-old protester told a reporter. "The president has been here for 30 years. Why?"[30] Rafat told the reporter he holds a master's degree in geology but is unemployed and lives in El-Marg, an impoverished neighborhood in Cairo. Under Mubarak's government, Rafat said, he could see no better future for himself.

Protest in Tahrir Square

Often translated as "Martyr Square" or "Liberation Square," Tahrir Square is a huge public place in the center of Cairo. The headquarters for Mubarak's political party are located across the street. As they planned the January 25 demonstration, organizers fully expected to be confronted by police. And so they sent out contradictory messages over social media designed to confuse police while instead making most of their plans through cell phone text messaging.

The tactic worked. Given the history of repression common in Egypt, organizers expected just a few hundred protesters to arrive in Tahrir Square. Instead, hundreds of thousands of people showed up—easily overwhelming the few thousand riot police dispatched to the square. Meanwhile, in Alexandria nearly 1 million people flooded into the Corniche.

In Tahrir Square the demonstration quickly turned rowdy. Demonstrators were able to break through police lines by linking their arms. Scuffles broke out as police officers beat some demonstrators. Some young men threw rocks at the police while other demonstrators turned over cars and set them on fire. The police fought back, firing rubber bullets into the crowd while also flinging tear gas grenades into the square. As protests broke up in one part of the square, though, activists galvanized into new groups in other parts, chanting "Freedom, freedom, freedom. Where are the Egyptian people?"[31]

After hours of such parrying between police and demonstrators, and as nightfall approached, Tahrir Square settled into an uneasy peace. In the square, protesters refused to leave—vowing to sleep in the square that night and remain until Mubarak left office. Some Egyptians were not sure the tactic would work. They fretted that Mubarak had found a way to remain in power for three decades and that he would ultimately lose patience with the dissidents. "I think it is the beginning of the process," Mustapha Kamel al-Sayyid, a political science professor at the American University in Cairo, told a reporter at the end of the first day of protests. "Some of the demonstrators are still in Tahrir and said they will not leave until their demands are met by the government. Their demands will not be met by the government, but they will not give up."[32]

Wael Ghonim

Wael Ghonim, the Egyptian computer engineer who helped established the "We Are All Khaled Said" page on Facebook, emerged as an unlikely hero of the Arab Spring. Unlike other dissidents who led marches and clashed with police, Ghonim used his knowledge of cyberspace to boost the revolution in Egypt.

Ghonim, an executive with Google, had been working in the United Arab Emirates when he learned of Said's death. "I just felt that we are all Khaled Said," Ghonim said. "That was a feeling. It wasn't just a brand name. It was a feeling. We were all of these young Egyptians who could die, and no one [would be] held accountable. So at the time, I thought, 'I have to do something.' And I believed that bringing Khaled's case to [the public] would be helpful."

Egyptian authorities soon realized Ghonim's importance in organizing the demonstrations. On January 27, 2011, he was quietly taken into custody. Eleven days later, as the end neared for the Mubarak regime, Ghonim was released. He went immediately to Tahrir Square, speaking from a stage to thousands of protesters. "We will not abandon our demand, and that is the departure of the regime," he said.

1. Quoted in National Public Radio, "Wael Ghonim: Creating a 'Revolution 2.0' in Egypt," February 9, 2012. www.npr.org.
2. Quoted in Theodore May, "Regime Won't Halt, but Rallies Must, Egypt's VP Says," *USA Today*, February 8, 2011. http://usatoday30.usatoday.com.

Similar protests occurred that day in other parts of Egypt. In Alexandria demonstrators tore down a huge portrait of the president. Moreover, that first day of protests resulted in three deaths. Authorities reported that one man in Cairo and two protesters in the city of Suez lost their lives in the scuffles.

Blaming the Muslim Brotherhood

Over the next four days, the protesters camped out in Tahrir Square under the nervous eyes of the police, who were under orders to keep their distance. By now the police had tried to change tactics, believing the best way to put down the demonstration was to block Internet access and disrupt cell phone communications. Police attempted to block microwave transmissions in the vicinity of Tahrir Square, which at times did disrupt cell phone communications. Also, the Egyptian police found a way to block access to Twitter, which many of the activists were using to communicate plans. Both these attempts proved to be short-lived; technicians at Twitter found a way to break through the Egyptian government's firewall, and the government's attempts to block cell phone communication ultimately failed as well.

Another tactic attempted by the regime to derail the protest was to blame it on radical Islamists—specifically, the Muslim Brotherhood. Government officials believed most Egyptians appreciated the secular society in which they lived and did not want to see Islamists take control of the government and establish law under the principles of the Koran. Most Egyptians saw through the ruse. Said Amr Hamzawy, research director of the Carnegie Middle East Center, a public policy group based in Beirut, Lebanon, "This was not about 'Islam is the solution.'"[33]

Friday of Rage

As the demonstrations in Tahrir Square moved past the first day, there were occasional flare-ups among crowd members and police officers—but major trouble did not start until January 28, a Friday. Organizers selected that day as the Friday of Rage, calling on all Egyptians to pour into Tahrir Square to show their solidarity against the Mubarak regime. On that day, as new waves of demonstrators entered Tahrir Square, many protesters broke their pledge of *silmiyya*—nonviolence—and lashed out at police. They burned police stations and attacked riot police standing guard at the square. Eight people were reported killed in the melees. Even so, heroes emerged—and from some unexpected places. During the confrontations, several police officers were cheered and hoisted onto the shoulders of the crowd when they threw down their weapons, stripped off their uniforms, and refused to take part in quelling the demonstrations.

Meanwhile, Friday of Rage demonstrations were held in other cities. The Corniche in Alexandria was again the scene of a mass protest. In the city of Minya, twenty thousand protesters marched to Ramses Square, where they tangled with police.

Protesters climb on tanks and block roads in celebration of the military's January 29, 2011, announcement that it would not fire on Egyptian citizens. Egyptians continued to rally in Cairo's Tahrir Square and elsewhere, calling on Hosni Mubarak to resign.

By the end of the day, tempers had cooled, but Mubarak would stoke the flames that night when he appeared on national television. Protesters had hoped Mubarak would announce his resignation—instead, he gave vague promises of democratic reforms and promised to sack some unpopular cabinet ministers. Reacting to the speech, protesters in Tahrir Square dug in and refused to observe a national curfew.

Camel Battle

On January 29 the tide turned decisively in favor of the protesters. The army arrived on the scene, and instead of clearing Tahrir Square, military leaders announced they would not fire on Egyptian citizens. Protesters celebrated by climbing onto tanks and other military vehicles, waving anti-Mubarak banners and posing for pictures and videos that were uploaded to the Internet. Mubarak's strategy of keeping the military out of Egyptian politics had backfired: The army felt no loyalty to him and instead vowed to protect the Egyptian people.

Mubarak tried one last tactic. In what would emerge as one of the most bizarre scenes of the Tahrir Square protest, on February 2 a group of thugs recruited by the regime entered the square, riding camels and horses. Wielding sticks, their intent was to intimidate and disperse the crowd, but the protesters held their ground and in many cases pulled the riders off their mounts. The hapless attackers were kicked and beaten by protesters. As many as fifteen hundred people—on both sides—were injured during the confrontations. "Today's violence is again an indication of a criminal regime that has lost any common sense," said Mohamed ElBaradei, a respected Egyptian legal scholar. "We have no intention whatsoever—at least I speak for myself on this—in engaging in dialogue with this regime until the number one person responsible for this, who is Mubarak, leaves the country. He must get out."[34]

After the so-called Camel Battle, the mood in the square remained tense. The police held their ground as many of the protesters fretted that the movement was losing its momentum. Within a few days of the battle, the number of protesters remaining in the square had dwindled to a few thousand. One protester, Noor Ayman, told a reporter, "I do not want to say this is lost, because if we had said that, for example, a week ago, or 10 days ago or a year ago, then we wouldn't be where we are today. I'm going to say things are a lot more difficult than they were a while back."[35]

Breaking Mubarak's Grip

Momentum returned to the protesters on February 7 when Wael Ghonim suddenly appeared in public. Ghonim had been secretly arrested and imprisoned on January 27. After his release he hurried to Tahrir Square and made a speech encouraging the people of Egypt to continue their support for the Tahrir Square protests. He blamed the deaths of protesters—by then nearly three hundred people had been killed in the clashes with police—on the Mubarak regime. The next day tens of thousands of protesters returned to Tahrir Square while hundreds of thousands of others flooded the streets of Cairo. Labor unions in Egypt called for a general strike; on February 10 they virtually shut down the country when workers refused to report to their jobs.

On February 11, the eighteenth day of the Tahrir Square protest, Mubarak announced his resignation from the presidency of Egypt. He had been forced out by the Supreme Council of the Armed Forces (SCAF), the council that heads the Egyptian military. Moreover, emissaries from the administration of Barack Obama had quietly made contact with Mubarak, urging him to leave before civil war broke out in Egypt.

Within months of his resignation, Mubarak and other members of his inner circle would go on trial, charged with numerous offenses against the nation of Egypt, including complicity in the deaths of protesters in Tahrir Square and other places where demonstrations had erupted. Among those in the regime who were arrested was Gamal Mubarak.

In 2012, Mubarak and others were convicted on the charges and sentenced to life in prison. Mubarack appealed the conviction and was granted a new trial, which convened in late 2013.

Egypt was now freed from the rule of a dictator whose iron grip on the country had been broken by a group of young dissidents who turned to social media to ignite a public uprising. Clearly, they had played important roles in the Arab Spring. These young dissidents were able to engage the citizens of Egypt who had suffered for decades under the tyrannical rule of one man. For now, the government was entrusted to the hands of SCAF leaders, who promised to keep peace until democratic elections could be held in 2012. In the months following the Tahrir Square protests, the people of Egypt looked with great optimism toward new lives under what many expected would be their first true democratic society.

Chapter 4

Death of a Libyan Dictator

Despite Libya's vast oil wealth, the people of the country's northeast province of Cyrenaica had known little but poverty. Dictator Muammar Gaddafi had long been wary of the people of Benghazi, Cyrenaica's largest city, believing them to be rebellious and unwilling to bend to his will. Gaddafi channeled little of the country's wealth to Benghazi, preferring instead to develop Tripoli as a cosmopolitan city featuring sports arenas, public parks, gardens, museums, and monuments. With widespread poverty and few opportunities for better lives, residents of Libya's second-largest city, Benghazi, openly grumbled about their supreme leader. Over the decades of Gaddafi's rule, the city evolved into a hotbed of dissension.

A measure of dissent in Benghazi could be found in the city's soccer stadiums. Soccer is by far the most popular sport in the Middle East. Knowing of the public's intense interest in the sport and the devotion fans show for their favorite clubs, Middle Eastern political leaders have been known to curry favor with clubs in order to gain their support. In Egypt Hosni Mubarak was known to fix the outcomes of soccer matches to favor clubs that had publicly endorsed his presidency.

In Libya Gaddafi secretly bought interests in several soccer clubs, most notably the club known as Al Ahly Tripoli, which was managed by his soccer-playing son Saadi. In 1996, when Saadi's team played in Benghazi, fans in the stadium started shouting antiregime slogans. To quiet the demonstrators, Saadi ordered his bodyguards to fire their guns into the crowd. Four people were killed by the gunfire. The incident prompted rioting outside the stadium where another fifty people were killed by police.

And so in January 2011, when protests against Muammar Gaddafi's rule first surfaced in Benghazi and other cities, he wanted to make sure dissidents could not use soccer matches to channel their hatred against him. Among the Libyan dictator's first acts to put down the revolt brewing against his regime was to cancel all soccer games.

The Cyrene Uprising

As the Arab Spring unfolded, events in Libya became known as the Cyrene Uprising because dissent first erupted in and near Benghazi. The people of Cyrenaica harbor an immense degree of national pride because the province was the home of Omar al-Mukhtar, a hero of the Libyan people who led a guerilla campaign against the Italian occupation in the 1920s.

Throughout the decades of his rule, Gaddafi seemed to make a special effort to infuriate the people of Benghazi. In 2000—in another confrontation during a soccer match—Al Ahly Tripoli played Al Ahly Benghazi in an important playoff game. In an act meant to insult Saadi's team, the Benghazi fans dressed a donkey in Al Ahly Tripoli colors and paraded the animal into the stadium. Muammar Gaddafi responded by sending bulldozers to Benghazi to demolish Al Ahly Benghazi's headquarters.

By then other cities in northeastern Libya, including Derna and Bani Walid, had also grown hostile to Gaddafi's regime. Although the impoverished citizens of the region were often instigators of street violence and other forms of protest, Gaddafi regarded his real enemy as a group of Islamic extremists—the Libyan Islamic Fighting Group, or LIFG. By the 1990s the LIFG was engaged in a virtual civil war against the regime. Its armed fighters adopted the guerilla tactics of al-Mukhtar, using the mountainous northeastern portion of the country to launch attacks against Gaddafi's soldiers. "There were reports of the army battling with LIFG members using helicopter gunships while the Islamists managed to kill scores of government security officers," says Ethan Chorin, a former US diplomat and foreign policy advisor to Barack Obama. "Benghazi residents recall the presence of military men with machine guns at intersections, barricades managed by [soldiers], all of which stood in stark contrast to the calm, controlled atmosphere in Tripoli."[36]

First Demonstrations

By early 2011 Tripoli may have been calm, but the same could not be said for Libya's closest neighbors. By then the tumultuous events of the Arab Spring had already surfaced in Libya's northwestern neighbor, Tunisia, where Zine al-Abidine Ben Ali had been driven from power. Meanwhile, the seeds of revolution had been planted in Libya's eastern neighbor, Egypt, where the death of Khaled Said would soon lead to the mass demonstrations in Tahrir Square against Hosni Mubarak's rule.

In public Gaddafi condemned the prodemocracy movements in Tunisia and Egypt. Two weeks after Ben Ali fled Tunisia, Gaddafi made a televised speech in Libya in which he suggested Ben Ali was a capable leader and warned Libyans the revolution in Tunisia would lead to new forms of tyranny. "Tunisia now lives in fear," he declared. "Families could be raided and slaughtered in their bedrooms and the citizens in the street killed as if it was the [Russian] or the American revolution."[37]

Indeed, evidence suggests Gaddafi was highly concerned that fervor for revolution could spill over into his country. In early January 2011, in an effort to bolster his army, Gaddafi assigned his son Khamis the job of procuring more weapons for the Libyan military. Khamis contacted several Western arms manufacturers but found no new sources of supply for his father's military.

The first demonstrations against Gaddafi's rule erupted in Benghazi on January 13 and 16. In most cases demonstrators gathered at abandoned construction sites, which they regarded as symbolic of their city's poor economy and Gaddafi's failure to improve their lives.

In February 2011 antigovernment protesters in Benghazi wave the Libyan flag and demand an end to Muammar Gaddafi's iron-fisted rule. Violence ensued as Libyan forces and hired mercenaries fired on protesters.

Opulent Lifestyles

As these demonstrations occurred, news reports surfaced chronicling the opulent and aloof lifestyles led by Gaddafi and the members of his family. His son Mutassim, for example, was reported to have paid $1 million to stage a private New Year's Eve party featuring performances by Beyoncé and Usher. Another son, Hannibal, was reported to have assaulted his wife in a hotel suite in London, drawing a measure of embarrassing press attention to the Gaddafi family. And as dissent spread throughout the Arab world, a third son, Saif al-Islam—believed to be the choice of his father to eventually head the government—appeared to be regarding his country's problems with an attitude of aloofness by leaving for a hunting trip in New Zealand. These revelations about Gaddafi's family members served to infuriate the poor people of Benghazi and other Libyan cities.

Denied weapons by Western arms manufacturers, Gaddafi knew it would take more than military strikes to put down the rebellion. He moved to quash dissent. On February 1, soon after Libyan journalist Jamal al Hajji appeared on TV and called for more protests, Gaddafi had him arrested. Two other dissidents, Taqi al Din al Chalawi and Abdel Fattah Bourwaq, who ran a politically charged website, were taken into custody on February 16. Soon after Benghazi journalist Idris al-Mismari contacted Al Jazeera to persuade the Qatar-based TV network to start covering the Libyan insurrection, he was arrested, tortured, and dumped onto a Tripoli street, where he was left for dead. He was found by friendly activists and given medical care.

Gaddafi also issued a warning to leaders of the uprising: He told them that he would hold them responsible if he was forced to resort to violence to put down dissent. The activists brushed off the dictator's warning and instead called for a mass protest for February 17 in Benghazi. "We knew we likely had a single shot, a limited window in which to cripple the regime," says Ibrahim Sahad, who helped organize the Benghazi protests. "If it failed, the blowback from the regime would be decisive. We would not have a second chance."[38]

In a final attempt to put down the February 17 demonstration, which protesters named the Day of Rage, Gaddafi tried a new tactic: He tried to buy off the people of Benghazi. On the morning of February 17, Saadi Gaddafi spoke on Benghazi radio, making an appeal for peace and promising to pump money into the impoverished city's economy. During his address to the people of Benghazi, Saadi promised that roads and other infrastructure would be repaired and that a new airport, estimated to cost $24 billion, would be developed for the city. That morning the man who once ordered his bodyguards to shoot into the crowd at a Benghazi soccer match told the people of the city he would personally guarantee their protection: "I have taken permission from my father so he can give me Benghazi, no one will come near it, I am coming to live there, I am even bringing my clothes . . . now we will give you all of what you want. I promise good money and whatever you want you will get. I will take care of the young people and the infrastructure."[39]

Chaos in Benghazi

By the time Saadi Gaddafi spoke on Benghazi radio, lawyer Fathi Terbil had already been arrested for his activism in representing the families of the Abu Salim prison massacre and his role in planning the Day of Anger protest. News of Terbil's arrest on February 15 spread quickly through Benghazi as well as other cities. By the morning of February 16, protesters had already started marching through streets in several cities. In the cities of Tobruk and Al Beida, clashes between demonstrators and police left four dead and about eighty injured.

On the next morning, soon after Saadi's radio address, the army sent armored vehicles through Benghazi streets. Muammar Gaddafi also hired mercenary troops from the African nation of Chad, and they were sent into the streets as well. As for the protesters, several thousand amassed in front of Al Manar, a landmark building that resembles a lighthouse, on the campus of the University of Benghazi.

Chaos ensued. Protesters clashed with the mercenaries and with Libyan army soldiers. Gaddafi's forces opened fire on the demonstrators; many jumped off the nearby Juliana Bridge into the Port of Benghazi to avoid gunfire. The violence continued for several more days as protesters returned to the Benghazi streets. On February 18, some six hundred people gathered in front of police headquarters in Benghazi, where several scuffles between dissidents and police erupted. Hundreds gathered at a town square in Benghazi known as Maidan Al Shajara; police arrived and dispersed them using water cannons. In retaliation, protesters burned several police stations.

One protester, forty-nine-year-old Mahdi Ziu, a father of two, filled his car with propane tanks and other explosives, then rammed the vehicle into the wall of a huge military compound known as the Katiba. Ziu's suicide mission blew a huge hole into the wall. Hundreds of demonstrators rushed into the compound and fought with soldiers. Many people were injured in the melee as well as in other incidents. From February 17 through February 20, Benghazi hospitals treated more than 2,000 injured protesters, 110 of whom died.

The Fate of Saif al-Islam Gaddafi

Saif al-Islam Gaddafi was believed to be his father's choice as the future leader of Libya. The holder of a doctoral degree in economics, Saif was given the job of attracting Western investment to the country. He also headed several Libyan charities organized by his father and was believed to be working behind the scenes to improve the Libyan government's record on human rights.

But when the rebellion broke out in Libya, Saif stayed intensely loyal to his father. On the night of February 20, 2011, Saif appeared on Libyan television and, instead of appealing for calm, gave a long and rambling speech that warned the insurgents of the bloodshed to come. "We will be mourning hundreds of thousands," he declared.

He was captured in November 2011 by rebels while trying to flee Libya and imprisoned in the city of Zintan. Visitors who have met with Saif report that he has lost three fingers, which they suspect were sliced off by his captors. By late 2013 he remained in custody, awaiting trial on human rights abuse charges.

Quoted in Ethan Chorin, *Exit the Colonel: The Hidden History of the Libyan Revolution*. New York: PublicAffairs, 2012, p. 197.

The Rebels Arm Themselves

When the demonstrators gained access to the Katiba, they made their way to the compound's armory, where they found guns and ammunition. At that point, the protests in Libya turned into something more than what had occurred in Tunisia and Egypt. There were moments of violence in those countries, but now, for the first time, Arab Spring dissidents had armed themselves. During the protests in Tunisia and Egypt, authorities in both countries managed to avoid outright civil war. In Tunisia and Egypt, Ben Ali and Mubarak both backed down, largely because they lost the support of their armies. That was not the case in Libya. At least during the early weeks of the protests in Benghazi and other Libyan cities, the army largely stayed loyal to Gaddafi. This made it possible for the Libyan dictator to use considerable force to repel the movement against his rule. And so in Libya, protesters believed they had no other alternative but to arm themselves.

In addition to the weapons seized at the Katiba, the first guns to fall into the hands of the insurgents may have also been supplied by defecting members of the Libyan army. However, throughout his long tenure as dictator of Libya, Gaddafi had often infuriated other Arab leaders with his support for terrorism as well as his brazen insults to their rule. Gaddafi once funded a bungled plot to assassinate King Abdullah of Saudi Arabia. So when the insurgency grew in Libya, its leaders found many allies elsewhere in the Arab world—Saudi Arabia, Qatar, and the United Arab Emirates are believed to have provided arms to the rebels.

Soon the insurgency spread to other Libyan cities. On February 23, rebels took control of Misurata, Libya's third-largest city. Gaddafi responded by dispatching the Libyan military, which surrounded the city. For months, Misurata would be shelled by Gaddafi's artillery, destroying many of the homes and businesses as well as the infrastructure of the city.

No-Fly Zone

Still, the insurgency grew. By late February many senior officials in the Libyan government had defected, among them Mustafa Abdel Jalil, minister of justice, and Mahmoud Jibril, Gaddafi's chief economist, both of whom resigned from Gaddafi's government on February 21. Jalil and Jibril organized the National Transitional Council (NTC), which would serve as the guiding hand of the insurgency and seek international legitimacy for the movement to overthrow the dictator. In response to the formation of the NTC, Gaddafi dug in and vowed to break the insurgency. He said he would seek out the rebels "*zanga zanga, dar dar*"—in English, "alley to alley, house to

Refugees from the besieged seaside city of Misurata load their belongings onto a truck after being evacuated by an international rescue organization's ship to the rebel-held seaport city of Benghazi. Gaddafi's forces shelled Misurata for months.

house." He also called the insurgents "rats" and "cockroaches."[40] This incendiary language served only to drive more Libyans into the ranks of the rebels.

On February 21 the insurgency scored a major victory when two Libyan air force pilots landed their fighters on the nearby island of Malta in the Mediterranean Sea. They had defected, telling the world they refused to follow Gaddafi's orders to strafe and bomb protesters in Benghazi. The incident led to a meeting of the United Nations Security Council, which feared Gaddafi was planning a massacre of his own people. On March 17 the Security Council adopted Resolution 1973, which established a no-fly zone over Libya. The resolution authorized foreign countries to use their militaries to ensure Libyan air force jets remained on the ground. Moreover, the Arab League, a political union composed of most of the Arab states, endorsed the United

Muammar Gaddafi held no official title in his government. He was usually referred to as supreme leader of Libya. He was just twenty-seven years old and a junior army officer in 1969 when he engineered a coup against the seventy-nine-year-old King Idris. At some point after seizing power in Libya, Gaddafi awarded himself the rank of colonel, and he was known to favor gaudy military uniforms.

He was born in 1942 near the town of Sirte to a family of nomads—for much of his early life, his home was a tent in the desert. Relations between Gaddafi's government and America had been tense since 1981, when two Libyan air force planes were shot down by US Navy planes over the Mediterranean Sea. The American pilots said the Libyans fired on them; they returned fire, easily downing Gaddafi's planes. In 1986 a bomb exploded in a German nightclub, killing three people in an attack evidently aimed at American servicemen—two of the victims were Americans. US intelligence agencies determined that Gaddafi's agents were behind the bombing, and in retaliation President Ronald Reagan ordered a military strike on Tripoli. Gaddafi escaped unharmed and always claimed he repelled the invaders, erecting a statue in front of his headquarters depicting a fist crushing a US fighter jet.

Nations resolution—thereby sending a message to Gaddafi that he had no allies within the leadership of the Arab world.

The first jets to enforce the no-fly zone were dispatched on March 18 by the French air force. They were soon joined by aircraft from the British and US armed forces. The US and British navies also set up a naval blockade of Libya, turning back ships suspected of smuggling weapons to Gaddafi's troops. Within a week the North Atlantic Treaty Organization (NATO), which is composed of the militaries of the US and most of the industrialized Western nations, took over enforcement of the no-fly zone, not only ensuring Gaddafi's planes would remain on the ground but also using their resources to attack the dictator's ground troops from above. NATO's intervention would have a devastating effect on Gaddafi's ability to carry out the war against his own people. Indeed, a NATO bombing mission is believed to have nearly killed the dictator, who evidently departed from the scene just minutes before the attack.

The Liberation of Libya

NATO's entry into the war provided the rebels with a decisive advantage. By late summer 2011 Gaddafi's forces were in retreat. The army suffered greatly from desertion, and the rebels received not only arms from Gaddafi's Arab enemies but on-the-ground intelligence and leadership as well. The Qataris, for example, are believed to have sent in military advisors and trainers to organize rebel assaults. Meanwhile, starting in July the rebels, working with NATO, began planning an assault on Tripoli.

On August 21 the first rebels entered Tripoli. They were met not with resistance by Gaddafi's troops but with the open arms of the Libyan people. Soon they surrounded Bab al-Aziziyah, Gaddafi's fortified compound in the city. Two days later Bab al-Aziziyah fell after a coordinated NATO air strike and ground assault by the rebels. Inside, the rebels found few Libyan soldiers left behind to guard the compound. As for Gaddafi, the dictator had slipped out a few days earlier.

Libya was now declared liberated. The NTC established a provisional government as the people of Tripoli, Benghazi, and other cities celebrated with wild street parties. But the rebels, knowing that Gaddafi remained at large, were still wary, fearing the crafty dictator could find a way to return to power. Says Chorin, "Libya was gripped by a powerful ambivalence: a sense of relief on the part of the rebels and most of the population that the regime was done, balanced by a foreboding that arose from the fact that Gaddafi—and most of his family members—were still at large."[41]

Gaddafi's Final Days

As for Gaddafi, his whereabouts would remain unknown for the next two months. A nationwide manhunt was organized. Most of the rebels' attention was focused on the city of Sirte—the place of Gaddafi's birth—which had remained loyal to the former dictator and still had not fallen into rebel hands.

Rebels pushed their way into Sirte and conducted street-by-street searches for Gaddafi. Rumors swirled throughout Sirte as well as other cities. Many rebel leaders believed Gaddafi may not have been in Sirte but instead hiding somewhere in the Libyan Desert, regrouping his supporters, gathering arms, and preparing for a new offensive.

As things turned out, Gaddafi was still in Sirte and was very much in hiding. The few supporters who stayed loyal had taken to foraging through abandoned houses, searching for food. Gaddafi was said to have lost touch with reality, spending hours wandering through the rubble of city streets babbling incoherently to family members he reached on his satellite phone.

On the night of October 19, Gaddafi's bodyguards realized the rebels were closing in on their hiding place and that they had perhaps just hours left before what would probably be their final confrontation. The bodyguards made the decision to try a predawn escape from the city. Their aim was to leave under darkness and find a place to hide in the desert. On the morning of October 20, 2011, a convoy of about one hundred vehicles began leaving the city. The convoy was spotted by a Nevada-based American intelligence team operating a Predator drone. The team relayed the sighting to NATO command, which alerted a French air force fighter. The fighter found the convoy and attacked. Just one or two cars in the convoy were hit and destroyed, but Gaddafi's bodyguards panicked and stopped their vehicles. Dozens of Gaddafi loyalists ran into the streets of Sirte, where they were quickly apprehended by rebels. Many of the loyalists were shot on the spot; others were rounded up and jailed.

As for Gaddafi, the dictator stumbled out of his car and hid in a sewer drain, where he was found by rebels. He was roughed up, dragged through the streets, kicked, slapped, and bloodied. Gaddafi's last words, before a rebel pointed a gun to his head and fired, were, "What did I do to you?"[42]

Libyans in Tripoli celebrate the October 2011 capture and death of Muammar Gaddafi. They rejoice at their liberation from four decades of oppressive rule.

The Arab world's most vindictive and dangerous dictator was now dead, his country liberated after more than four decades of oppressive rule. The Arab Spring in Libya lasted longer and was much bloodier than the uprisings in Tunisia and Egypt. According to the NTC, by the time the fighting ended, as many as thirty thousand Libyans may have lost their lives. Given the relatively small population of the country—just 6 million people—this loss represented a significant portion of the citizenry. As the Arab world was soon to learn, though, the death of Gaddafi would not mean an end to the bloodshed.

Chapter 5

What Are the Legacies of the Arab Spring?

The uprisings of the Arab Spring went beyond Tunisia, Libya, and Egypt. During 2011 and beyond, nearly every Arab nation was touched by protests. Some ended in regime change: In Yemen, for example, dictator Ali Abdullah Saleh was chased out of power after he was injured in a bomb blast at the presidential compound in the capital city of Sana'a. As in Libya, Saleh had waged war against his own people but was forced to resign by his neighbors on the Arabian Peninsula—most notably the Saudis, who hold considerable influence in the Arab world.

In Jordan King Abdullah responded to demonstrations in his country by agreeing to widespread democratic reforms, giving more power to the office of the prime minister. In the past Abdullah had handpicked the prime minister, but now the head of the Jordanian government would be selected by the national legislature—and therefore indirectly through the votes of Jordanians.

Even Oman, a desert kingdom of about 4 million people, was touched by protests. There, protesters usually numbered in the hundreds rather than the thousands. Oman is an oil-rich monarchy that has been ruled for more than forty years by a sultan, Qaboos bin Said. Over the years Oman has been a model of stability in the Arab world. Nevertheless, from January through May 2011, many poor Omanis marched in the capital of Muscat and other cities to demand higher wages as well as other reforms. "We love His Majesty, but there are problems we want to fix,"[43] said Maan al-Miaani, a twenty-four-year-old bank teller who took part in a protest in the city of Sohar.

In response to the protests, Qaboos agreed to a series of reforms, including unemployment benefits as well as a job-creation plan sponsored by the national government. Qaboos also created elected municipal councils to act as advisory panels. Although Qaboos still maintains final authority over the direction of his country, creation of the advisory panels and the other reforms indicate the sultan's willingness to give his people a voice in their government.

Crackdown in Bahrain

Other Middle Eastern monarchs were less generous than Qaboos. In Bahrain, a tiny island nation in the Persian Gulf with a population of little more than 1 million, demonstrators took to the streets in the capital of Manama on February 14, 2011. They gathered at a familiar landmark—the Pearl Roundabout, a circle in downtown Manama that featured the Pearl Monument, a public sculpture that included a globe towering high above the city.

The Bahraini protesters hoped to camp out in the Pearl Roundabout as the Egyptian dissidents had made camp in Tahrir Square. Bahraini king Hamad bin Isa bin Salman Al Khalifa would show little patience for the protests. Two days after the demonstrators arrived at the Pearl Roundabout, the king dispatched police to break up this act of defiance.

Soon violence broke out throughout the country. As demonstrators took to the streets, it was estimated that half the country's population had joined the protest. On March 14 the king called on his close allies, the Saudis, who supplied troops. The Saudi soldiers entered the Pearl Roundabout, demolishing the center of the protest movement and destroying the monument. Says Barack Obama's foreign policy advisor Marc Lynch, "The crackdown . . . quickly became one of the most comprehensive, brutal, and oppressive of any in the region."[44]

Civil War in Syria

In Bahrain about one hundred protesters are believed to have lost their lives in the clashes with police and Saudi soldiers. In nearby Syria a much more substantial loss of life was suffered by the rebels who sought to force longtime dictator Bashar al-Assad from power.

Assad has led the nation since 2000, when he ascended to power following the death of his father, Hafez al-Assad, a dictator who ruled the country of 22 million people for thirty years. As with other citizens of Arab states, Syrians endured the heavy hand of a police state as well as official corruption that left many citizens mired in poverty. The first protests in the Syrian capital of Damascus were staged on January 26, 2011. At first, Assad tolerated the protests, but in March fifteen young Syrians—some as young as nine—were caught by police writing anti-government slogans on a wall in the city of Dara'a. The police reacted harshly, throwing all the young people in jail.

Rows and rows of tents provide temporary shelter for Syrian refugees in northern Iraq in 2013. The office of the UN High Commissioner for Refugees (UNHCR) is among the agencies that have tried to help millions of Syrians who have fled their country's civil war.

Gains for Women in the Arab States

Women have made some gains in Arab politics, but progress has been slow. The most important gain for women is the elimination—or at least the modification—of quota systems that restricted how many women could run for office. In Tunisia, for example, women are guaranteed at least half the places on all ballots for public office. Egypt eliminated a quota restricting women to just 64 of 518 seats in the national legislature; now women may run for all seats in the assembly.

Yet despite the changes, women in Arab countries have seen mixed results. In Tunisia by 2013, four of six important legislative committees were headed by women, but in Egypt women held just 2 percent of the seats in the legislature. In an essay written for the international public policy group the EastWest Institute, Meg Munn, a member of the British parliament, argues that as women feel more empowerment, they will make new gains. "The experience they have obtained pushing for collective, national goals has been invaluable," she says. "They cannot be legislated away or removed from an individual's memory. This experience of coming together to be agents of positive change has become a seed that will grow into greater demands for women's rights."

Meg Munn and Nicole Cleminshaw, "Has the Arab Spring Been Beneficial for Women?," East-West Institute, March 28, 2013. www.ewi.info.

The jailing of the young people stunned local residents, and protests soon broke out. On March 20 hundreds of demonstrators marched through the streets of Dara'a, chanting, "There is no fear, there is no fear, after today there is no fear!"[45] The protesters were met by police, who opened fire on the crowd, killing three protesters.

The killings in Dara'a sparked massive protests throughout Syria. At first, Assad seemed apologetic—he sent his condolences to the families of the dead protesters and ordered the release of the jailed boys. But the incident empowered dissidents, who called on Syrians to rise up and oust Assad from power. The country soon lapsed into civil war as rebel groups armed themselves and engaged in bloody street battles with Assad's troops. By 2013 there seemed to be no end in sight to the conflict that engulfed the Arab nation. At the time, the death toll in Syria stood at more than one hundred thousand. Moreover, 2 million Syrians had fled their homes, taking refuge in the neighboring countries of Lebanon and Iraq.

Unlike the civil war in Libya, by 2013 the rebels had not received significant aid from Western countries. The US government has acknowledged supplying small arms to rebel groups, but the United Nations had not imposed a no-fly zone over the country, nor had NATO stepped in as a peacekeeping force. In the case of Syria, diplomats from America and other Western countries believe that the rebellion is too fragmented—meaning it has no clear leadership—and that it is likely Islamic extremist groups are taking part in the uprising. American diplomats fear providing arms to the extremists because if they are successful in toppling Assad, it is likely they will establish a government hostile to America and other Western nations. In 2012 US Army general Martin Dempsey, chair of the Joint Chiefs of Staff and therefore the highest-ranking officer in the American military, made this comment about the situation is Syria: "Syria today is not about choosing between two sides but rather about choosing one among many sides. . . . It is my belief that the side we choose must be ready to promote their interests and ours when the balance shifts in their favor: Today, they are not."[46]

Meanwhile, Assad seemed to have no qualms about using whatever weapons he could find to quell the uprising. In August 2013 reports surfaced that Assad had used chemical weapons against insurgents in a suburb of Damascus, Syria's capital city, killing nearly 1,500 people.

Elections in Egypt

Despite the unsettled situation in Syria, many rebels believe it is possible to bring democracy to a nation that has been ruled by dictators for more than forty years. Says Ribal al-Assad, director of the Organization for Democracy and Freedom in Syria, a British-based human rights group:

> Syrians have experienced uninterrupted dictatorship for forty years, and, with it, extreme economic hardship, including high unemployment, rising food prices, and endemic corruption. . . . But Syrians are a remarkably resilient, resourceful people, as well as being young and well educated. . . . We can build a robust civil society that can assert its own identity and sovereignty, independent of undue outside influence. A new Syria, based on democratic principles, would not only benefit Syrians, but would be a force for stability throughout the region.[47]

Whether Syria can make the transition to democracy remains to be seen. Other Arab Spring nations have encountered significant difficulties on this same road. In Egypt, after Mubarak's ouster, the army took control of the country and eventually scheduled elections. In June 2012 Egyptians voted in their first truly democratic election. The results stunned the world when the populace elected as president Mohamed Morsi, a member of the Muslim Brotherhood, the organization of Islamic fundamentalists virtually outlawed by Mubarak.

During the political campaign, Morsi promised to govern fairly, but some Egyptians and many outside observers feared Egypt would fall under the control of radical Islamists should Morsi win the election. Nevertheless Morsi was victorious, winning 51.3 percent of the vote to 48.7 percent cast for Ahmed Shafiq, a Mubarak loyalist. At first, Egyptians were exuberant with the outcome of the election, declaring that in their country democracy had finally prevailed. "[The election] is a revolution against the very nature of the Arab state that is not accountable to its people," said Khaled Fahmy, a history professor at the American University in Cairo. "For the first time, we have the people in the largest Arab country having and dictating their say."[48]

Morsi's Brief Presidency

Morsi soon fell short of the task of forging a true democracy in Egypt. Soon after taking office he attempted to assume a degree of dictatorial power, scrap the constitution, and adopt a body of laws based on Islamic doctrine. His presidency lasted just a year. In July 2013, amid growing protests by Egyptians who returned to Tahrir Square, the army forcefully removed him from power. Morsi's embrace of Islamic

President Mohamed Morsi speaks in Cairo shortly after his June 2012 election. A year later, acting on fears that he intended to impose Islamic doctrine on the secular government, Egypt's military removed Morsi from power.

Exchanging Radical Ideas in Tunisia

During the dictatorship of Zine al-Abidine Ben Ali the free expression of ideas was suppressed as part of the president's campaign against dissent. In the years following Ben Ali's overthrow, many veterans of the Jasmine Revolution gather at the Théâtre de l'Étoile du Nord—the North Star Theater—in Tunis. There they freely discuss politics, the arts, and anything else on their minds. The theater is, actually, more of a café than a theater—it has no stage and patrons sit at tables watching performances staged in the aisles. Among the patrons are students, political activists, and gay Tunisians who under the old regime avoided congregating in public out of fear of oppression.

The theater is located in the same neighborhood as the Interior Ministry, headquarters of Ben Ali's once-feared police. The theater's owner, French-trained actor Noureddine El Ati, says free societies need places where people congregate to air ideas. He believes that under Ben Ali, such open thought was suppressed for so long that it finally exploded in rage, leading to the dictator's downfall. "People who are abandoned, without a project, for whom the state does nothing and who are lost—they have to do something or they become aggressive," he says.

Quoted in Carlotta Gall, "A Café Where the Spirit of the Arab Spring Lives On," *New York Times*, August 7, 2013, p. A-8.

law worried Egyptians who feared he would turn away from secular governance. Moreover, during his year in office Morsi had done little to address Egypt's widespread problems of poverty, corruption, and unemployment. By the summer of 2013, the Egyptian army announced plans to stage new elections in 2014.

But Morsi's ouster calls into question the issue of whether elements of Egyptian society—including the Egyptian army—are prepared to accept democracy. Despite the policies he espoused, Morsi was elected in a democratic process. If Morsi had been elected in a Western democracy, his removal from office by any means other than through the next election would be unthinkable. And yet when protests erupted against his administration, and the Egyptian army leadership concluded that Morsi intended to govern under the principles of fundamentalist Islam, his removal from office was carried out quickly and decisively.

Jeffrey Goldberg, a commentator on international politics for Bloomberg News Service, says, "Morsi was freely and fairly elected. If the anti-Morsi demonstrators had exhibited patience . . . they would, theoretically at least, have had their chance to remove him at the ballot box."[49] Goldberg adds, however, that by scuttling the Egyptian constitution and governing as an Islamic fundamentalist, it was becoming clear to democracy advocates in Egypt, as well as to army leaders, that Morsi may have sought to cancel the next elections and rule very much in the style of the dictator he replaced. "A number of [Egyptian] friends have written to me . . . arguing that what the Egyptian people did—or what the Egyptian army, responding to the will of the people, did—was to forestall the rise of a new Hitler," says Goldberg. "The analogy is overdone, but it is true that the Brotherhood is a totalitarian cult, not a democratic party."[50]

Soon after Morsi was removed from power, Egypt erupted in mass demonstrations as his supporters, mostly members of the Muslim Brotherhood, took to the streets. Army leaders sent in troops, and for several days it appeared as though Egypt teetered on the brink of civil war. The army eventually prevailed, although about one thousand people were killed in the violent clashes.

Fears of Extremism in Tunisia and Libya

Tunisia has managed to avoid the bloodshed found in Syria, Egypt, and Bahrain, but the country's path to democracy has also been rocky. After democratic elections in December 2011, the new president, Moncef

Marzouki, pledged to govern over a secular society. But in 2013 the country was rocked by the murders of two of Marzouki's political opponents, Chokri Belaid and Mohamed Brahmi. American foreign policy observers note that Marzouki's political party, Ennahda, is dominated by Islamists, prompting fear that secularism in Tunisia will give way to Islamic law. Indeed, in 2013 the government ordered the daytime closures of restaurants and coffee shops during the holy month of Ramadan—a gesture that did not sit well with many Tunisians who believe the government has no business telling them how to observe Islam.

Moreover, many Tunisians complain that Marzouki and his party have done little to address the concerns that led to the ouster of Zine al-Abidine Ben Ali: the poverty, lack of opportunity, and corruption that is widespread in their country. A 2013 national poll showed 78 percent of Tunisians are dissatisfied with Ennahda, suggesting that a new popular uprising may be in Tunisia's future. And on August 21, 2013, thousands of protesters gathered outside the national assembly building in Tunis and demanded Marzouki resign and new elections be scheduled. The protest remained peaceful.

Libya has made strides toward democracy, but Western observers believe there is still cause for concern. Elected president in 2013, Nouri Abusahmain won in a close vote of 96–80 in the country's national legislature. Abusahmain won with the support of Islamists, prompting foreign policy experts to fret that the new president may govern as Morsi attempted. Soon after his election, however, Abusahmain promised to preside under the spirit of the 2011 revolution. Still, foreign policy experts find the situation in Libya unsettling. On September 11, 2012, violence erupted in Benghazi when armed Libyans attacked the US consulate, killing four people, including US ambassador J. Christopher Stevens. The attack has been blamed on Islamic extremists, fueling the argument that Libya remains a volatile corner of the Arab world that could fall into the grip of terrorists.

Setback for Islamists

Although Western observers fear a rising influence of radical Islamists in the Arab states, the failure of Morsi to govern has, in the eyes of

Proud voters show off the ink marks that prove they voted (and that prevent multiple voting) in Tunisia's October 2011 national election. Women voters for the first time have spoken or will speak in other parts of the Arab world.

many observers, proved that Arab peoples will not trust their fates to Islamists. Says Fawaz Gerges, a Middle East analyst for the London School of Economics, "What happens in Egypt has a major impact. . . . I am not talking about the loss of power, but the setback to the moral argument that the Islamists somehow stand above the fray, and are more competent. In fact, one of the lessons we learned is that they are as incompetent, if not more so, than the old authoritarian regimes."[51]

Indeed, those who may have benefited the most from the Arab Spring are people who traditionally enjoy few rights under Islamic law: Arab women. Under conservative interpretations of the Koran, women often have fewer rights than men, although different Arabic cultures have granted women varying degrees of rights. In Saudi Arabia, for example, it is illegal for women to drive and to vote, although women will have voting rights beginning in 2015. Moreover, Saudi women must always wear the hijab—the traditional head covering. Saudi women also may not live on their own—they must be sheltered either by their fathers, brothers, or husbands. In more cosmopolitan Jordan, however, women may be elected to parliament, and they need not wear veils or other head coverings. Still, in Jordan women must have the permission of their husbands to work.

The Arab Spring empowered Arab women to seek new rights. Women were very much a part of the protests in Tahrir Square in Cairo as well as in other Arab cities. Says Egyptian journalist Mona Eltahawy, "They realize that, if they can stand up to Mubarak, they can stand up to their fathers and their mothers and their brothers. . . . They realize that there's a Mubarak in every home."[52] And so as new legislative bodies begin drafting constitutions in Arab nations, women have insisted that their rights be expanded so they enjoy suffrage, employment opportunities, and freedom from oppression by male society.

New Drive for Pan-Arab Unity

Perhaps the most lasting legacy of the Arab Spring, though, is a renewed drive toward pan-Arab unity—a notion that died out during the squabbles and treachery of the Nasser years. In the wake of the Arab Spring, many Arabs have realized they may be divided by national borders, but they are united by common goals. As people gathered on the streets of cities throughout the Arab world, they demanded similar rights: to be recognized as citizens, to have their votes count, to be given opportunities for education, employment, and advancement enjoyed by citizens of Western nations. Says Marc Lynch:

> This unified narrative of change, and the rise of a new, popular pan-Arabism directed against regimes, is perhaps the greatest revelation of the uprisings. Not since the 1950s has a single slogan—back then Arab unity, today "The People Want to Overthrow the Regime"—been sounded so powerfully from North Africa to the [Persian] Gulf. This identification with a shared fate feels natural to a [younger] generation.[53]

The peoples of the Arab world may have a long way to go before they achieve the goals of the Arab Spring. As President Obama noted in an August 2013 speech, "In that part of the world, there are ancient sectarian differences, and the hopes of the Arab Spring have unleashed forces of change that are going to take many years to resolve."[54] The democracies that emerged in the wake of the Arab Spring are shaky. Moreover, Islamic extremists have felt empowered by the ouster of dictators, although the failure of the Muslim Brotherhood to form an effective government in Egypt has discredited their cause. It may be many years before a new Arab world emerges, but there is no question that change has come to the Middle East and North Africa, and a new and young generation of leaders will decide the fate of the Arab peoples.

Source Notes

Introduction: The Defining Characteristics of the Arab Spring

1. Marc Lynch, *The Arab Uprising: The Unfinished Revolutions of the New Middle East*. New York: PublicAffairs, 2012, p. 13.
2. Ali Hashem, "The Arab Spring Has Shaken Arab TV's Credibility," *Guardian* (London), April 2, 2012. www.guardian.co.uk.
3. Natana J. Delong-Bas, "Insight: Women of the Arab Spring, Beyond Objects and Subjects," Middle East Voices, January 29, 2013. http://middleeastvoices.voanews.com.

Chapter One: What Conditions Led to the Arab Spring?

4. Milton Viorst, *Sandcastles: The Arabs in Search of the Modern World*. New York: Knopf, 1994, p. xi.
5. T.E. Lawrence, *Seven Pillars of Wisdom*. Reprint, New York: Penguin, 1979, p. 218.
6. Lawrence, *Seven Pillars of Wisdom*, pp. 23–24.
7. Lynch, *The Arab Uprising*, p. 25.
8. Nick Turse, "Obama and the Mideast Arms Trade," TomDispatch, May 17, 2011. www.tomdispatch.com.
9. Quoted in Nazila Fatah, "In a Death Seen Around the World, a Symbol of Iranian Protests," *New York Times*, June 23, 2009, p. A-1.

Chapter Two: Tunisia's Jasmine Revolution

10. Quoted in Edward Cody, "Tunisian President, 'Senile,' Is Removed by His Deputy," *Washington Post*, November 8, 1987, p. A-1.
11. Quoted in Nicolas Marmie, "Tunisia's Political Machine Looks to Sweep Elections," *Memphis Commercial Appeal*, October 25, 2004, p. A-6.

12. Quoted in Ian Black, "An Uncriticised Success," *Guardian* (London), November 7, 2007. www.theguardian.com.

13. Quoted in Phyllis Meras, "My Naïve Travels in Tunisia, Before It Boiled Over," *Seattle Times*, January 19, 2011. http://seattletimes.com.

14. Meras, "My Naïve Travels in Tunisia, Before It Boiled Over."

15. Quoted in Lin Noueihed and Alex Warren, *The Battle for the Arab Spring: Revolution, Counter-Revolution and the Making of a New Era*. New Haven, CT: Yale University Press, 2012, p. 74.

16. Quoted in John Thorne, "Free at Last, Tunisians Tell Their Stories of Life Under Ben Ali," *National* (Abu Dhabi, United Arab Emirates), January 26, 2011. www.thenational.ae.

17. Quoted in Thorne, "Free at Last, Tunisians Tell Their Stories of Life Under Ben Ali."

18. Quoted in Thorne, "Free at Last, Tunisians Tell Their Stories of Life Under Ben Ali."

19. Quoted in Thorne, "Free at Last, Tunisians Tell Their Stories of Life Under Ben Ali."

20. Quoted in Yasmine Ryan, "How Tunisia's Revolution Began," Al Jazeera, January 26, 2011. www.aljazeera.com.

21. Quoted in Ryan, "How Tunisia's Revolution Began."

22. Quoted in Yasmine Ryan, "Tunisia's Bitter Cyberwar," Al Jazeera, January 6, 2011. www.aljazeera.com.

23. Quoted in Noueihed and Warren, *The Battle for the Arab Spring*, p. 75.

24. Quoted in William Maclean, "Tunisia Army Pivotal to Ben Ali Ousting," Reuters, January 17, 2011. www.reuters.com.

25. Quoted in Susan Perry, "The Saudi Arabian Quagmire: Ben Ali, Mubarak and Impunity," *Debating Human Rights* (blog) American University of Paris, February 1, 2011. http://debatinghumanrights.org.

Chapter Three: Eighteen Days That Changed Egypt

26. Quoted in Miret El Nagger, "Protests Erupt in Egypt over Suspicious Death," *South Florida Sun Sentinel* (Fort Lauderdale), June 26, 2010, A-9.

27. Quoted in Kareem Fahim, "Death in Police Encounter Stirs Calls for Change in Egypt," *New York Times*, July 19, 2010, p. A-4.

28. Quoted in Associated Press, "Egypt's Elections: Opposition Alleges Fraud," *Guardian* (London), November 29, 2010. www.theguard ian.com.

29. Alaa Al-Aswany, "Observations on the Gamal Mubarak Project," *World Affairs Journal*, August 31, 2010. www.worldaffairsjournal .org.

30. Quoted in Kareem Fahim and Mona El-Naggar, "Violent Clashes Mark Protests Against Mubarak's Rule," *New York Times*, January 25, 2011, p. A-1.

31. Quoted in Fahim and El-Naggar, "Violent Clashes Mark Protests Against Mubarak's Rule."

32. Quoted in Fahim and El-Naggar, "Violent Clashes Mark Protests Against Mubarak's Rule."

33. Quoted in Fahim and El-Naggar, "Violent Clashes Mark Protests Against Mubarak's Rule."

34. Quoted in Jack Shenker, "Egypt: Violence Means Talks with Mubarak Regime Are Out, Says ElBaradei," *Guardian* (London), February 2, 2011, p. 6.

35. Quoted in Philip Williams, "Standoff on the Streets of Cairo," Australian Broadcasting Corporation, February 2, 2011. www.abc.net .au.

Chapter Four: Death of a Libyan Dictator

36. Ethan Chorin, *Exit the Colonel: The Hidden History of the Libyan Revolution*. New York: PublicAffairs, 2012, p. 55.

37. Quoted in Matthew Weaver, "Muammar Gaddafi Condemns Tunisia Uprising," *Guardian* (London), January 16, 2011. www.the guardian.com.

38. Quoted in Chorin, *Exit the Colonel*, p. 190.

39. Quoted in Chorin, *Exit the Colonel*, p. 192.

40. Quoted in Noueihed and Warren, *The Battle for the Arab Spring*, p. 180.

41. Chorin, *Exit the Colonel*, p. 254.

42. Quoted in Noueihed and Warren, *The Battle for the Arab Spring*, p. 187.

Chapter Five: What Are the Legacies of the Arab Spring?

43. Quoted in Thomas Fuller, "Rallies in Oman Steer Clear of Criticism of Its Leader," *New York Times*, March 1, 2011, p. A-8.

44. Lynch, *The Arab Uprising*, p. 111.

45. Quoted in Rania Abouzeid, "Syria's Revolt: How Graffiti Stirred an Uprising," *Time*, March 22, 2011. www.time.com.

46. Quoted in Bradley Klapper, "No Change Seen in U.S. Syria Policy," *Philadelphia Inquirer*, August 22, 2013, p. A-5.

47. Ribal Al-Assad, "Struggle for Democracy in Syria," *Sunday Times* (London), August 14, 2011. www.sundaytimes.lk.

48. Quoted in Charles Levinson, Matt Bradley, and Tamer el-Ghobashy, "Islamist Wins Egyptian Vote," *Wall Street Journal*, June 25, 2012. http://online.wsj.com.

49. Jeffrey Goldberg, "In Egypt, a Win That Is Also a Loss," *Philadelphia Inquirer*, July 7, 2013, p. C-2.

50. Goldberg, "In Egypt, a Win That Is Also a Loss," p. C-2.

51. Quoted in Paul Schemm, "Reverberations for Islamists: Egypt's Overthrow Instills Caution," *Philadelphia Inquirer*, July 8, 2013, p. A-2.

52. Quoted in Wendell Steavenson, "Two Revolutions," *New Yorker*, November 12, 2012, p. 32.

53. Marc Lynch, "The Big Think Behind the Arab Spring," *Foreign Policy*, December 2011, p. 46.

54. *New York Times*, "Text of President Obama's Remarks on Syria," August 31, 2013, www.nytimes.com.

Important People of the Arab Spring Uprisings

Rachid Ammar: The head of the Tunisian army may have been the person who told Zine al-Abidine Ben Ali he was through as president. When Ben Ali ordered Ammar to fire on protesters in Tunis, Ammar refused. Ammar knew his army was small and ill equipped and may have been concerned that in a street battle, his soldiers would lose. In any event, Ammar chose country over president.

Bashar al-Assad: The Syrian dictator has held power since 2000, taking office following the death of his father, Hafez al-Assad, who ruled the country of 22 million people for thirty years. Assad has used harsh tactics to put down the demonstrations that erupted in his country in 2011; since then Syria has been embroiled in a civil war that has cost about one hundred thousand lives.

Zine al-Abidine Ben Ali: The Tunisian dictator seized power in 1987, turning Tunisia into a one-party state in which the opposition was crushed, ordinary citizens were abused by police, and conservative Muslims jailed out of fear they would join a revolution. He was chased from power in January 2011 after losing the support of the Tunisian army.

Mohammed Bouazizi: On December 17, 2010, police confiscated Bouazizi's fruit cart. After years of abuse at the hands of the police, the twenty-six-year-old street vendor could endure their treatment no longer. In the ultimate act of protest, he drenched himself with paint thinner and lit a match. His death touched off the events that would lead to the fall of dictators throughout the Arab world.

Muammar Gaddafi: The quirky and eccentric army officer seized power in Libya in 1969, becoming one of the Arab world's most dangerous and vindictive dictators. As protests engulfed the city of Benghazi in 2011, Gaddafi refused to step down, and civil war erupted. When Western military powers came to the aid of the rebels, he was chased from power and killed by rebels while on the run.

Saadi and Saif al-Islam Gaddafi: These two sons of Muammar Gaddafi would become the focal points of Libyan hatred. Saadi once ordered his bodyguards to shoot unfriendly fans at a soccer game in Benghazi; later his father asked him to make an appeal to the city for peace. Saif was groomed to take over the Libyan government; when violence started he warned that thousands would die in the insurrection.

Wael Ghonim: One of the activists who created the "We Are Khaled Said" page on Facebook, the Google executive used his cyberskills to plan the January 25, 2011, demonstration in Cairo's Tahrir Square. Knowing of his importance to the democracy movement, Egyptian police quietly arrested Ghonim on January 27 but released him days later as the regime neared collapse.

Mustafa Abdel Jalil and Mahmoud Jibril: Jalil, minister of justice in Libya, and Jibril, the country's chief economist, were the two top officials to defect to the side of the Libyan rebels. They established the NTC to oversee the rebellion, giving the rebels credibility in the international community. The NTC helped convince the United Nations to establish a no-fly zone over Libya.

Hamad bin Isa bin Salman Al Khalifa: The king of Bahrain endured no protests in his country. Soon after protesters gathered in the capital of Manama, the king sent in police to break up the demonstrations. When half his country's population took to the streets to protest, Khalifa summoned troops from Saudi Arabia, who broke up the movement for democracy violently and decisively.

Mohamed Morsi: Egypt's first democratically elected president held office for just one year. A member of the Muslim Brotherhood, Morsi promised to preside over a secular government but soon after taking office attempted to scrap the constitution and implement Islamic principles. After protesters returned to Tahrir Square in July 2013, the army removed Morsi from office.

Hosni Mubarak: The vice president of Egypt ascended to the presidency in 1981 following the assassination of Anwar El Sadat. Mubarak turned Egypt into a virtual police state as he used his powers to stamp out dissent while also amassing a personal fortune of $70 billion by looting his national treasury. He was ousted in Arab Spring protests in February 2011.

Khaled Said: In June 2010 the twenty-eight-year-old activist for democracy in Egypt was dragged out of an Alexandria Internet café and beaten to death by two police officers. The assault was captured by cell phone images and uploaded onto the Internet, where the incident alerted the world to the cruel tactics of the Egyptian police and sparked widespread support for the ouster of Hosni Mubarak.

Fathi Terbil: The Libyan lawyer and human rights activist agreed to represent the families of the inmates slain in the Abu Salim prison massacre. He also helped organize public demonstrations in Benghazi. When Muammar Gaddafi had Terbil imprisoned, his arrest sparked public protests in Benghazi.

Mahdi Ziu: Ziu's suicide mission to blow a hole in the wall of the Libyan army compound known as the Katiba helped turn the popular uprising into a civil war. After Ziu's car blew a hole in the wall, activists rushed into the compound, found the armory, and armed themselves. The activists now had weapons to use against Muammar Gaddafi's troops.

For Further Research

Books

Ethan Chorin, *Exit the Colonel: The Hidden History of the Libyan Revolution*. New York: PublicAffairs, 2012.

Paul Danahar, *The New Middle East: The World After the Arab Spring*. New York: Bloomsbury, 2013.

Alcinda Honwana, *Youth and Revolution in Tunisia*. London: Zed, 2013.

T.E. Lawrence, *Seven Pillars of Wisdom: A Triumph; The Complete 1922 Text*. Blacksburg, VA: Wilder, 2011.

Marc Lynch, *The Arab Uprising: The Unfinished Revolutions of the New Middle East*. New York: PublicAffairs, 2012.

Lin Noueihed and Alex Warren, *The Battle for the Arab Spring: Revolution, Counter-Revolution and the Making of a New Era*. New Haven, CT: Yale University Press, 2012.

Nasser Weddady and Sohrab Ahmari, eds., *Arab Spring Dreams: The Next Generation Speaks Out for Freedom and Justice from North Africa to Iran*. New York: Palgrave Macmillan, 2012.

Carrie Rosefsky Wickham, *The Muslim Brotherhood: Evolution of an Islamist Movement*. Princeton, NJ: Princeton University Press, 2013.

Websites

Al Jazeera (www.aljazeera.com/watch_now). The Qatar-based TV network offers an English-langue version of its website. Users can find updates on news as it is covered in the Arab world. By accessing the link for "Human Rights," students can find many stories on how activists are bringing changes to countries that for decades were governed as police states.

Human Rights Watch (www.hrw.org). The New York City–based human rights group provides commentaries by foreign policy experts and videos of newsworthy events in the Middle East and North Africa. Visitors to the site can download the group's report *Challenges for Rights After Arab Spring*, in which Human Rights Watch lists the tasks the new Arab governments must carry out to ensure democracy.

Inside the Arab Awakening (http://freevideolectures.com/Course/2972 /The-Institute-of-Politics/5). Presented by the Kennedy School of Government at Harvard University, the site provides an eighty-minute video of a Febraury 2013 panel discussion at Harvard covering the Arab Spring. The panel features four scholars who discuss the events that led to the Arab Spring and provide their thoughts on whether the Arab nations will be able to establish sustainable democracies.

Muslim Brotherhood (www.ikhwanweb.com). The Muslim Brotherhood's English-language website provides viewpoints from the perspective of the Islamic group, which believes Arab nations should be governed under the principles of the Koran. The site includes many commentaries by Muslim Brotherhood leaders insisting that the ouster of Mohamed Morsi was unconstitutional and that the brotherhood will eventually prevail.

Organisation for Democracy and Freedom in Syria (www.odf-syria .org). Based in Great Britain, the organization tracks human rights abuses in Syria—a significant task, given the death toll in a country in the throes of civil war. The group's website includes news reports and videos that chronicle the conflict. Under the link for "Key Issues," students can read about the group's position on women's rights, freedom of the press, and democratic elections.

Path to Protest (www.theguardian.com/world/interactive/2011/mar/22 /middle-east-protest-interactive-timeline). Maintained by the *Guardian* newspaper of London, the site provides an interactive timeline of events during the Arab Spring. The site highlights events in seventeen countries in the Arab world; users can select a country and access *Guardian* stories about events in that nation.

US Department of State Background Notes (www.state.gov/r/pa/ei /bgn). The State Department serves as the chief diplomatic service for the federal government. The agency's "US Bilateral Relations Fact Sheet Webpage" provides a menu of dozens of countries, including those in the Arab world. By accessing each country, students can find a summary of the country's political situation as well as the state of its relations with the American government.

"We Are All Khaled Said," Facebook (www.facebook.com/elshaheeed .co.uk). Long after the fall of Hosni Mubarak, activists have maintained the "We Are All Khaled Said" page on Facebook, which can be accessed by non-Facebook members. The page has become an online meeting place for activists in a number of Arab countries who post news, photos, and videos of the democracy movements throughout the Middle East and North Africa.

Index

Picture Credits

About the Author

Hal Marcovitz is a former newspaper reporter and columnist. He is the author of more than 150 books for young readers. His other titles in the World History series include *Ancient Rome*, *Ancient Greece*, and *The Industrial Revolution*.